OPEN TO NEW LIGHT

Quaker Spirituality in Historical and Philosophical Context

Leslie Stevenson

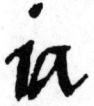

imprint-academic.com

Copyright © Leslie Stevenson, 2012

The moral rights of the author have been asserted.
No part of this publication may be reproduced in any form
without permission, except for the quotation of brief passages
in criticism and discussion.

Published in the UK by
Imprint Academic, PO Box 200, Exeter EX5 5YX, UK
Published in the USA by
Imprint Academic, Philosophy Documentation Center
PO Box 7147, Charlottesville, VA 22906-7147, USA

ISBN 9781845402303

A CIP catalogue record for this book is available from the
British Library and US Library of Congress

Table of Contents

	PREFACE	v
1.	A SEVENFOLD SPIRITUAL QUEST	1
2.	THE PHILOSOPHY OF SOCRATES	9
	Ancient Athens in the 5th century BCE	9
	The life and death of Socrates	10
	Our sources of knowledge about Socrates	12
	Socrates' philosophy	13
	A few comments on Socrates' philosophy	20
3.	THE TEACHING OF JESUS	23
	Ancient Jewish society up to the time of Jesus	23
	The sources of our knowledge of Jesus	27
	Jesus's teaching	31
	Some comments on Jesus's teaching	42
4.	ANCIENT PHILOSOPHIES OF LIFE	45
	A world of multicultural empires	45
	Plato	46
	Aristotle	48
	Epicureanism	50
	Stoicism	51
	Roman stoicism	53
5.	RATIONALISM OR FUNDAMENTALISM: RECURRING TENSIONS IN CHRISTIANITY, ISLAM AND JUDAISM	59
	Christianity—the first three centuries	59
	The Council of Nicea	65
	The Trinity, the Holy Spirit, and Eastern Orthodox Christianity	67
	Muhammad and the birth of Islam	70
	Medieval Islam	73
	Medieval Judaism	77
	Christian scholastic theology	80

6. GEORGE FOX AND THE BEGINNING OF THE QUAKERS ... 85
   The Reformation ... 85
   17th-century England ... 87
   George Fox's Light of Christ Within ... 89
   The beginning of the Quaker movement ... 93
   Fox's religious ethics ... 94
   The growth of Quakerism ... 98

7. LIGHT OR ENLIGHTENMENT? ... 103
   Inward light? ... 103
   Robert Barclay's "immediate revelations" and Descartes' "natural light" ... 104
   Fallibilism in identifying the Light or Spirit ... 109
   Locke on "enthusiasm" and "reason" ... 111
   The Enlightenment ... 113

8. KANT'S PHILOSOPHY OF RELIGION COMPARED
   TO QUAKERISM ... 117
   Kant's philosophy ... 117
   Does the Religious Society of Friends exemplify
       Kant's ethical community? ... 120
   How far do Quakers and Kant agree on theology? ... 123
   Do Kant and Quakers differ on the possibility of religious experience? ... 130

9. GOD AS METAPHOR ... 135
   Is it a matter of existence? ... 135
   Conceptions of God in the Bible and the *Qur'an* ... 137
   Personification in the arts ... 140
   Personification in theology ... 141
   God-talk without personification ... 143
   Farrer on poetic truth ... 145
   Metaphorical realism in theology? ... 149

10. RESURRECTION? ... 157
    Dogma and openness in religion ... 157
    What is resurrection of the body supposed to be? ... 160
    The resurrection of Jesus? ... 165
    Resurrection as spiritual renewal ... 168
    Wittgenstein and an epistemology of love? ... 173

    INDEX ... 179

Preface

This book is about "the meaning of life" or "the spiritual quest". I offer a selective and critical evaluation of some strands of Western religious and philosophical thought over two millennia and more, together with some recommendation of the kind of approach I have found in the Quakers. But I am not setting out to convert my readers to Quakerism, though obviously I think that is one good way and community in which to pursue the spiritual quest. Nobody can come to these topics with a blank mind, but that does not mean one has to approach them with a *closed* mind, a mind already firmly made up and unwilling to listen to anything that does not fit with one's preconceptions. I hope to demonstrate, and to appeal for, an openness of mind to new light, and perhaps to offer some refreshed insights into eternal questions and venerable traditions.

Knowledge of how traditions have developed over many centuries can help us understand how the options now on the market have reached their present form. I start with Socrates' philosophy of life, and I survey the amazing development of philosophy that he initiated in ancient Greece. I offer my own take on the teaching of Jesus, and on the tangled history of Christianity in the two millennia since his time. I also explore the history of Judaism and Islam, since these religions share roots and similarities with Christianity and have interacted with it in important ways.

In the early modern period, I devote a chapter to George Fox and the beginning of the Quaker movement, and I go on to discuss its relation to the Enlightenment. I suggest that there are some surprising parallels between the undogmatic spirituality of the Quakers and the heavyweight philosophy of religion of Immanuel Kant.

In the penultimate chapter, I recommend a non-literal interpretation of language about God, with some help from Austin Farrer on "poetic truth". And in the last chapter I extend this approach to the concept of resurrection, making use of some of Wittgenstein's striking remarks about the topic.

I am writing for the intelligent general reader — someone who would like an approach to these most basic issues of human life that is accessible but not dumbed down, an approach that is reliably knowledgeable but not overburdened with detail, critically argumentative but not (I hope) prejudiced. There are thousands of "general reader" books on religion and spirituality on the market. This one is different from those that are committed in advance to orthodox credal Christianity (though I am not hostile to it, either), and also from those that offer some kind of "new-age" spirituality, perhaps with vaguely Eastern connections.

Chapter 8 has been adapted, with the permission of the publishers, from my article "Kant's Approach to Religion compared with Quakerism", in *Kant and the New Philosophy of Religion*, ed. Chris L. Firestone & Stephen R. Palmquist (Bloomington: Indiana University Press, 2006).

CHAPTER 1

A SEVENFOLD SPIRITUAL QUEST

In this introductory chapter I am going to approach the idea of "spiritual quest" from a secular or humanist starting-point, and take the discussion to a point from which we can go on to ask what various philosophies and religious traditions have to offer.

There are at least three main ways in which human life transcends the biological existence that we share with the other animals. Firstly, there is our conscious relation to time: we "look before and after", as Shakespeare put it—unlike Burns's "wee, sleeket, cowran, tim'rous beastie" whom "only the *present* toucheth". We can remember past experiences, and we have emotions based on them: we experience nostalgia or relief, we may feel resentful or thankful about what someone has done, and we can express our anger or gratitude in words or actions. We can foresee the future to some extent, so we do some things that bring no immediate reward: we take exercise or medicine for the sake of our health, we pay insurance premiums, and we save money for the future. All these are matters of *prudence*, i.e. individual self-interest in the medium to longer term.

Some tricky questions can be asked even at this first level. *Which* aspects of one's own future should one be concerned about? *How much* "thought for the morrow" should one take? Jesus said "Do not be anxious about tomorrow; tomorrow will look after itself" (*Matthew* 6:34), but that surely does not exclude all forward planning, otherwise no crops would get sown, no pension funds would be invested, and no children would get educated. So how far should one be spontaneous and enjoy the present moment, trusting to God or providence or the state to provide, and how far should one take prudent concern for one's future?

At a second level, there is the whole business of our relationships to other people—the subject of *morality*. Prominent among our reasons for action (and forbearance from certain actions) are the effects on other people. We do things for our family or friends that we would not do for anyone else. We sometimes act for the sake of a wider community or institution, such as our village hall, our favourite sports team, a club or fraternity, church, school or university, a regiment, or even a corporation. In wartime people do things for their nation, and occasionally someone refuses military service with the interests of wider humanity in mind. Moved by reports and pictures of human suffering, we sometimes donate to charities and disaster relief funds anywhere in the world.

Morality thus involves reasons for action that transcend prudent self-interest and family (gene-based) interest. Sometimes we do things not because we hope to benefit thereby, but because we feel that it is the only right thing to do in the situation—for example, keeping a promise however inconvenient it is, handing in a lost wallet to the police, telling the truth even when it is to one's disadvantage, giving to a beggar on the street, stopping to help an accident victim, defending a stranger from robbery or rape, or sticking through difficulties in a marriage for the sake of the children. (Isn't it a disturbing sign of the times that so many of these examples have a somewhat old-fashioned ring?)

But *which* effects on other people should one be concerned about? What is the practical content of the commandment to "love one's neighbour as oneself"? How far can one, and *should* one, devote oneself to the good of other people? Jesus said "Sell all that you have, and give to the poor"—but are we supposed to follow that quite literally, and thus become one of the poor ourselves? How much should one give to the poor, then? And to *which* of the many millions of poor that we are made aware of in this globalized world? Now that major climate change threatens, questions about our obligations to *future* generations are becoming especially pressing. But how far can we, and should we, take into account the needs of people yet unborn, perhaps at the cost of those presently alive? The teaching of Jesus, or Confucius or the Buddha, expresses a spirit of unselfishness and generosity in which to approach these questions, but does not give detailed answers.

At a third level, beyond prudence and morality, there are *ideals*, things that we care about for their own sake. What is the point of foregoing present pleasure unless there are some things one wants to be or do later on, things that make life worth living because one sees them as intrinsically worthwhile? This is another crucial aspect that distinguishes us from other animals: we have values and ideals that go beyond survival and reproduction. Except in our most deprived, exhausted or depressed moments, there are always some things to be enjoyed, or projects to be pursued for their own sake. Examples include devotion to sport whether as participant or supporter, listening to music or playing an instrument, walking in the country, pursuing professional advancement, enjoying life with one's long-term partner, bringing up one's children, commitment to a political campaign or a religious community, or building an empire. Getting rich is an obvious project for many, but it can hardly count as an end in itself, for it can always be asked what one wants riches *for*?

There is a two-way relationship between morality and ideals. What is the point of taking other people into account unless those lives have some purpose beyond mere survival? We may admire the Mother Teresas of this world, but it would be strange (and surely impossible), if everyone were always occupied in trying to help other people. There had better be some things which people find worth doing or being, to give point to others helping them. In that sense our ideals transcend morality. The term "ethics" (often equated to "morality") could be usefully reserved for the wider combination of all three aspects of life that we have distinguished here, namely prudence, morality, and ideals.

Conversely, morality places limits on what people may care about. The mere fact that someone thinks something important does not give them license to pursue it irrespective of its effects on others. Aristocratic landowners have had whole villages removed to improve the view from their grand houses, and empire-builders of every sort ride roughshod over those who get in their way. Some of the political movements and religious cults that arouse the most enthusiastic devotion are found by others to be morally questionable or repugnant. Even with harmless hobbies like fishing, collecting stamps, playing golf, learning the guitar, or supporting a football team, questions can be asked about the amount of time and resources spent on them—as spouses or partners usually do! There is no project or ideal that we can safely say is beyond morality, for we can always ask which things are *worth* devoting attention to, and how much. If someone comes to care, to the detriment of much else in his life, about completing his collection of the stamps of Ruritania, or not stepping on the cracks in the paving stones, or keeping his hands superbly clean, he is acting irrationally. (Obsessive-compulsive disorders can be life-disabling.) Less extreme cases are more typical, when someone cares too much about one thing and not enough about another—e.g. about professional or sporting or social success rather than the well-being of his or her children (remember Thackeray's Becky Sharp).

But who is to say what is *too* much? Most options have to be a matter for individual choice. Expert (or supposedly expert) advice is offered these days on many matters—investments, insurance, medical procedures, health and safety, and even counselling on life-style—but in the end each person has to decide which advice to follow or ignore. There is a variety of lives, interests and temperamental inclinations, no one of which is obviously best. People vary in their attitude to risk, and a society in which everyone was terribly prudent might be boring indeed.

While there is universal agreement about some moral rules, such as the commandments forbidding murder, robbery and rape, others have come to be questioned. Is adultery *always* wrong? Or is it *as* wrong as the others? After all, it is not treated as a crime (not in Britain, anyway). Some moral issues have been hotly disputed in recent times, such as abortion, homosexuality, stem cell research, and pacifism; and various interest groups campaign noisily to enshrine their particular values in the law of their land. But in the absence of general consensus on such moral issues, it seems wise to maintain legal toleration, so that individuals can follow their own consciences.

For each person, then, the following three questions arise:

1. What is prudent, for myself?
2. What is morally required of me, in my relations with other people?
3. What do I believe is ultimately worth being or doing?

In trying to answer these questions, we should take into account the best of everything we can learn from others, but in the end we each have to take responsibility for our own decisions, even if they involve accepting the guidance given by a certain tradition. For the questions can always be asked: Why follow *this* tradition? And *which* features of the tradition should be maintained, and which should be reformed or dropped?

Admittedly, not many people explicitly ask such very general questions. But we all have to live our lives in one way or another, guided by values that usually remain implicit. And in our times of transition or crisis, such questions may arise quite consciously: for example in teenage or student years when people emerge from their family and schooling, in a "mid-life crisis", or when death approaches (remember Tolstoy's Ivan Illich).

In so far as we have some answer, whether explicit or implicit, about what to aspire to at each of the three levels, a further set of practical questions arises, namely, how can we live up to those standards? It is one thing to accept or endorse a rule or ideal in principle, but quite another to follow it consistently in practice. Human nature is notoriously weak, as so many philosophers and religious teachers have noted down the ages.

How then is prudence to be learned and cultivated? (And how can those who worry and fret *too* much allow themselves to live more in the present?) How can virtue be taught, developed and encouraged? This is a classical question, central to the thought of the Greek philosophers Socrates, Plato, and Aristotle, and of course to other traditions such as Confucianism and Buddhism. And how can we come to care less about things that do not matter, and care more about the things that matter most? ("Teach us to care and not to care", wrote T.S. Eliot.) Perhaps that is what is involved in the Jewish and Christian commandment to love God with all your mind, all your heart and all your soul.

The notion of rationality or reason, often held up as distinctive of humanity, and much-trumpeted by the philosophers of ancient Greece and of the 18th-century Enlightenment, does not give us much guidance as to what is ultimately worth aiming at, which of our desires are to be encouraged and developed, and which should be suppressed or transformed. Some people can be highly intelligent and ruthlessly efficient in action, yet utterly selfish, perverse, or even evil in the aims they pursue. The notion of love is more promising as a general guide, but it is ambiguous, so we need to be clear about what sort of love is presented as ideal. C.S. Lewis distinguished four kinds, putting *agape* (the Greek word in the New Testament for divine or divinely-inspired love, traditionally translated as "charity") on a different level from the three merely human, potentially imperfect, loves—namely erotic desire, parental caring, and friendship. Freud thought the Christian ideal of *agapé* impossible for humans to live up to, but even that eloquent old 19th-century pessimist Arthur Schopenhauer recognized the possibility of ascetic renunciation of self as one way that human beings can escape the almost universal domination of biologically-based "will" (the other way of transcendence he recognized was through aesthetic experience, especially music).

We have now arrived at a viewpoint from which we have distinguished six aspects of the spiritual quest, namely discerning the right *standards* at each of the three levels, and developing in ourselves the mental or spiritual *resources* to meet those standards. The number six becomes the mystic seven if we add in the choice of a community or tradition within which to pursue one's spiritual quest. Though individual decisions and effort are essential, we cannot rely on raising ourselves by our own bootstraps of mental energy or will-power, for all too often that is precisely where we find ourselves lacking. We typically need help from outside ourselves. If we are fortunate, it may come from friends or family, or from a teacher, a minister or a therapist, but as Christian tradition puts it, we are ultimately dependent on the grace of God. I will touch on that difficult concept later, but whatever it means, it can presumably be mediated through other people, and through religious traditions (or so one might hope).

The various religions and mind-developing or psychotherapeutic schools offer a wide choice of mental or spiritual practices. They have a number of different descriptions of the process—"self-improvement", "character-building", "growing in wisdom", "spiritual growth", "meditation", "pursuing mindfulness", "seeking enlightenment", "growing in grace", "entering the Kingdom of God". Questions about the meaningfulness and truth of the theoretical assumptions or theology of each school of thought can of course be raised. But the practical test is arguably more important: do their adherents show the "fruits of the spirit" listed by St. Paul in *Galatians* 5:22, namely love, joy, peace, patience, kindness, goodness, fidelity, gentleness, and self-control?

And there is another test that I suggest is worth applying, namely— is the tradition itself in a state of spiritual quest? Too many of them seem fixated on the past, requiring uncritical acceptance of a creed or sacred scripture (or a particular interpretation of it), or of the authority of an institution or a particular charismatic leader. But traditions need not be set in stone, and indeed they *cannot* really be, for they have to adapt to new situations, whether they acknowledge them as new or not. I respectfully suggest that we can ask of any philosophical or therapeutic or religious tradition whether while respecting and learning from its past, is it open to *new* light? Does it continue to encourage and aid its adherents to grow in self-discipline, maturity, wisdom, and unselfish love, as society goes through successive waves of change?

Here then are the seven questions I have distinguished:

1. Prudence—how much should we care about our own individual futures?
2. Morality—in what ways should we care about other people?
3. Ideals—what is worth aiming at for its own sake?
4. How can we live up to the standards in 1?
5. How can we live up to the standards in 2?
6. How can we live up to the standards in 3?
7. What community or tradition should we join, to aid us in 1–6?

With these sorts of question in mind, let us start looking at some ancient and modern religions and philosophies of life.

For further reading

My talk of ideals has been influenced by Harry G. Frankfurt's essay "The Importance of What we Care About", *American Philosophical Quarterly* volume 15 (1978), reprinted in his collection with the same title (Cambridge: Cambridge University Press 1988). Although published in a professional philosophical journal, this essay is readable (with patience and concentration!) by non-philosophers. The same is true of Frankfurt's more recent short book *The Reasons of Love* (Princeton: Princeton University Press 2004).

Ideals can also be counted among the things we love (as Frankfurt notes), and many centuries ago St. Augustine wrote eloquently and influentially about how our attitudes to life are shown in what we love, for better or for worse. As an introduction to his thought, see Bonnie Kent's essay "Augustine's Ethics", in *The Cambridge Companion to Augustine*, edited by Eleonore Stump and Norman Kretzmann (Cambridge: Cambridge University Press 2001); or Ch. 5 "Will, love and right action" of John M. Rist, *Augustine* (Cambridge: Cambridge University Press 1994), especially the sections on love of God and love of neighbour.

C.S. Lewis's classic little book *The Four Loves* (HarperCollins reissue 2002) is a more easily readable introduction to the topic.

Amongst many books on "the Meaning of Life", there is that by Terry Eagleton in Oxford University Press's Very Short Introduction series (2008).

Some readers may be disappointed that I do not explore any Eastern traditions in this book. This is not because I do not rate them highly, but because I lack sufficient knowledge and experience. However, I can recommend the excellent short introductions to Confucianism, Hinduism and Buddhism by David Haberman in our joint book *Twelve Theories of Human Nature*, 6th edition (New York: Oxford University Press 2012).

CHAPTER 2
THE PHILOSOPHY OF SOCRATES

Ancient Athens in the 5th century BCE

Before we look at Jesus, let us go back about five centuries earlier to the beginnings of the other great source of Western culture. Ancient Greece was not a unified state but a number of self-governing cities that developed rival versions of their common culture. Greek religion was based on the polytheistic gods with Zeus as their chief, in whose honour the Olympic Games were held every four years. The Greeks also revered the oracle at Delphi, where a priestess pronounced obscure messages believed to come from the sun-god Apollo. The two great epic poems attributed to Homer—*The Iliad* and *The Odyssey*—held position of authority for the Greeks almost like that of the Pentateuch for the Jews (though that is to compare two very different cultures, as we shall see).

In the 5th century BCE the city-state of Athens became dominant. It had become prosperous through its widespread trade, it had led the Greeks in repelling invasion by the Persians, and a powerful navy enabled the Athenians to build up a maritime empire. They also developed a remarkably democratic system of government, in which every male citizen could attend the assembly and vote on political decisions (though eloquent speakers like Pericles gave leadership). The Greek word for city-state, *polis*, is the root of our words 'politics', 'political' and 'politician'.

Athens was also the centre of unprecedented intellectual advances. In the arts, the creations of Athenians rank with anything else in human history in architecture (the time-damaged facade of the Parthenon still dominates Athens), sculpture (Phidias), drama (Aeschylus, Euripides and Sophocles), and the writing of history (Herodotus and Thucydides). Early Greek theorists such as Thales and Pythagoras started research into the nature of the material world, and their combination of reasoning and observation is the basis of modern science. And philosophy—rational open-minded inquiry into the nature of reality and the purpose of human life—was started from almost nothing by a truly remarkable trio of Athenian geniuses, Socrates, Plato, and Aristotle.

These philosophers of world-historical importance emerged from a culture in which there was already a spirit of free, competitive inquiry about anything and everything. Some Greek thinkers had offered natural explanations of observed phenomena which tended to subvert traditional religious stories about the gods. But other philosophers concentrated more on human affairs. The "Sophists" were self-styled experts who offered, for a fee, to teach certain kinds of skill especially the art of rhetoric (persuasion by public speaking) which was crucial for political advancement. (They might be described as the public relations consultants of their time!) The Greek word *sophia* means wisdom, and the ambiguous legacy of the Sophists is shown by its two English derivatives 'philosophy' (love of wisdom) and 'sophistry' (the use of clever words to confuse or to deceive).

The Sophists could hardly avoid discussing questions of ethics and politics. Athenians had become aware of the variety of beliefs and practices in the Greek city-states and other cultures around the Eastern Mediterranean, so it was natural for them to ask whether there is any criterion of truth in these matters. Some of these thinkers expressed scepticism about whether moral and political values were anything more than arbitrary conventions; indeed Protagoras is credited with one of the first great philosophical one-liners: "Man is the measure of all things". What we now call "cultural relativism" was thus a tempting option at this early stage of thought.

The life and death of Socrates

One of Athens' most controversial figures was the ethical philosopher Socrates (469–399 BCE). He was neither a nature-philosopher (a proto-scientist) nor a Sophist. He did not take fees (how he made his living, we do not know!) he simply engaged in argument with any Athenian who was interested to take part. He served with distinction as a soldier, and had to take a small role in public affairs when his name came up for office by lot, but otherwise he kept out of politics. What he is remembered for is the unprecedented seriousness and intellectual rigour of his discussions of ethics, which set a new standard for all subsequent philosophy to follow. His great inspiring idea was that we can come to know the right way to live, if only we use our reason properly. He has been called the founding father of philosophy, not so much for any particular results he reached (typically his dialogues—as dramatized by Plato—end inconclusively), but for pioneering the method of using rational argument in personal dialogue in an open-minded, non-dogmatic way.

Socrates accepted what he took to be divine guidance from the oracle at Delphi, and from his own internal "voice". He did not explicitly oppose traditional Greek religious beliefs, yet he came under suspicion for unorthodoxy. At the end of the *Phaedrus*, Plato attributes to him a rather beautiful prayer whose words may not be his, but which seem very much in keeping with his spirit:

> O dear Pan and all the other gods of this place, grant that I may be beautiful inside. Let all my external possessions be in friendly harmony with what is within. May I consider the wise man rich. As for gold, let me have as much as a moderate man could bear and carry with him.
> (*Phaedrus* 279c)

In the last years of his long life, Socrates found himself in the middle of a very disturbed period. Athenian imperial pride and rivalry with their powerful Greek neighbours in Sparta led to the thirty-year Peloponnesian War, which ended in disastrous defeat for Athens, and a brief period of tyranny. When democracy was restored, Socrates came under suspicion because some of the people he had been associated with had taken part in that tyrannical violence. He was brought to trial in 399 BCE on a charge of subverting the state religion, inventing new gods, and corrupting the young. After eloquently conducting his own defence, he was condemned to death and had to drink the paralysing poison, hemlock. Ever since he has been revered as a martyr to philosophy.

Socrates was not the first Greek to get into trouble for questioning the basis of traditional religion. In a previous generation Anaxogoras was indicted on a charge of impiety for describing the sun as mass of stone on fire, and he only escaped death by flight. Protagoras, one of the most famous of the Sophists, was reported as saying "With regard to the gods I know not whether they exist or not, or what they are like. Many things prevent our knowing: the subject is obscure, and brief is the span of our mortal life." As a result, the Athenian Assembly banished him, and ordered his writings to be burnt. Even the great playwright Euripides was indicted for impiety, and chose exile at the age of seventy-two. As we will see in subsequent chapters, fear of subversion of the established order has been characteristic of many societies all down history. "Freethinkers" who question the validity of traditional beliefs and practices have all too often come to a sticky end. What is remarkable of ancient Athens is the quantity and quality of free thought that it encouraged, and the example it set has resonated down history ever since.

Our sources of knowledge about Socrates

Socrates did not leave any writings, so we have to depend on secondary sources for our knowledge of him. Of these, by far the most important are the dialogues written by Plato, who became the next great philosopher and the first to leave behind a substantial volume of written work. His dialogues are in conversational form, with Socrates usually taking the leading part. Most scholars think that in the earliest of these works Plato was showing Socrates' method in action on the sorts of ethical topics that Socrates himself had discussed. (The usual list of "Socratic" dialogues includes the *Apology, Euthyphro, Crito, Charmides, Laches, Lysis, Euthydemus, Protagoras* and *Gorgias*.) The *Phaedo* depicts Socrates on the very day of his execution arguing passionately and intricately for the immortality of the soul, but it seems that Plato was there putting his own theories into the mouth of Socrates.

There are some less interesting *Memorabilia* of Socrates by the soldier and landowner Xenophon, who makes it hard to understand why Socrates should have become so controversial (he is even represented as giving advice on estate-management!). Socrates also makes a cameo appearance as a figure of ridicule in Aristophanes' comedy *The Clouds*. This shows that he was already known for his eccentricities, such as getting so rapt in thought that he forgot his surroundings. He is said to have been ugly, but fascinating. He acquired a reputation for enduring hardship as a soldier, and for being able to hold his drink.

We cannot be certain that anything Plato wrote represents the actual words of the historical Socrates. Just as in the case of Jesus, we have only the writings of a later generation to rely on, and we have to interpret them in the light of what we know about the ancient Greek and Jewish cultures in which those two extraordinarily impressive individuals lived, taught, and met their deaths.

Socrates' philosophy

The dialogue known as the *Apology* vividly dramatizes Socrates' speeches in his own defence, when he was put on trial at the age of 70 before a jury of several hundred fellow-Athenians. Do not be misled by the title, for in this text Socrates does not apologize for anything, but strenuously explains and defends his lifetime practice of public philosophical inquiry: he is an "apologist" in the other sense of the word, i.e. someone who defends a position by argument.

Socrates first rejects the slanders that had sullied his reputation and which he presumes motivate the case brought against him. In the popular mind, he was "a wise man, a student of all things in the sky and below the earth, who makes the worse argument the stronger", and who "does not even believe in the gods" (18c). He says, however, that he has taken no part in such nature-philosophy, and that he has never taken a fee for his teaching.

How then, did he acquire a reputation for wisdom? He recounts the story of how a friend of his asked the oracle at Delphi if any man was wiser than Socrates, and the priestess replied that nobody was wiser. Puzzled by this message, which it seems he genuinely believed was of divine origin, Socrates wondered what it could mean. So he took to "examining", by persistent question-and-answer, some of those Athenians who had the highest reputation for wisdom, but he was disappointed to find that though they *appeared* wise to many (especially to themselves!) they were not really so wise at all. Socrates concluded that the oracle was right in this sense: that at least he was *aware* of his own ignorance on important matters, whereas no one else was. They thought they knew, but he was wiser in that he was under no illusion that he knew (21d). So he carried on what he took to be his god-given mission to engage his fellow-Athenians in philosophical dialogue about their manner of life: typically their pretensions to knowledge were deflated, and they got angry with him. We can well imagine that some of the younger generation enjoyed witnessing this intellectual sport, so that Socrates acquired a reputation for leading them astray.

Socrates now proceeds to the formal charge against him, which had three parts: "corrupting the young, not believing in the gods the city believes in, but in other new spiritual things" (24b). (It may seem alien to us now that the law could be invoked against unorthodox religious belief. We have got used to the idea of the separation of religion and state; but it was not always thus, and in some places it still isn't.) His moral seriousness comes out very clearly when he says:

> It would be wrong to think that a man who is any good at all should take into account the risk of life or death; he should look to this only in his actions, whether what he does is right or wrong, whether he is acting like a good or a bad man. (*Apology* 28b)

He goes on to say that to fear death is to think one knows what one does not know, since for all we know, death may be the greatest of all blessings (29a). Later on, after his death sentence has been pronounced, he says that either death results in non-existence, or in transition to another place where the dead exist, with the chance to keep company with those famed in previous generations, so in neither case is there anything to fear (40c).

Socrates imagines the court offering a sort of plea-bargain, that they will acquit him if only he will agree to stop annoying them by his philosophical questioning—but he contemptuously dismisses any such idea:

> Men of Athens, I am grateful to you and I am your friend, but I will obey the god rather than you, and as long as I draw breath and am able, I shall not cease to practise philosophy, to exhort you and in my usual way to point out to any one of you whom I happen to meet: Good Sir, you are an Athenian, a citizen of the greatest city with the greatest reputation for wisdom and power; are you not ashamed to possess as much wealth, reputation and honours as possible, while you do not care for nor give thought to wisdom or truth, or the best possible state of your soul? (*Apology* 29d)

He goes on to compare his divine function to that of a gadfly that is needed to sting into action a great and noble, but sluggish, horse (30e). (But such annoying flies run the risk of being swatted!)

Socrates also mentions his "divine or spiritual sign"—which was something quite distinct from the Delphic oracle. Apparently since his youth he had sometimes heard a voice warning him not to do something he was about to do, although it never positively encouraged him to any action (31d). This voice kept him out of politics (very wisely, one might think!), but it never discouraged him from philosophy. Perhaps it was Socrates' belief in this "divine sign" that led to the charge of inventing new spiritual beings.

He concludes the *Apology* by saying "it is the greatest good for a man to discuss virtue every day", and he summed up with his most-quoted one-liner: "The unexamined life is not worth living for men" (38a). (Story has it that the actress said to the philosopher "The unlived life is not worth examining"—but surely *both* statements could be equally valid!) Socrates' practice was based on actual person-to-person dialogue, in the belief that that was the best way to get people to think for themselves and perhaps change their approach to life. His faith was that we can, by the proper use of our faculty of reason, both come to realize what is good, and actually become good ourselves.

In Plato's other "Socratic" dialogues we are given many artfully-written examples of the Socratic method at work. One of the shortest is the *Euthyphro*, in which Socrates gets involved in a discussion of what piety is, something Euthyphro claims to be quite certain about. Socrates seeks an explicit general definition of piety that will cover all the admitted instances of it, and Euthyphro conspicuously fails to satisfy him. It is difficult, however, to interpret the central concept, usually translated as "piety". Our English word now has connotations of insincerity ("putting on a show of piety"), but this is not a feature of the Greek dialogue. The most famous line is when Socrates asks whether what is pious is loved by the gods because it is pious, or is it pious because it is loved by the gods? (10a). In a modernized form of this challenge, philosophers ask theologians whether what is good is made good simply by God's decreeing it to be so (with the implication that He could, if He so decided, make anything whatsoever count as good), or whether God, in declaring something to be good, is recognizing an objective, pre-existing standard of value? Is God a potentially arbitrary tyrant, or is goodness independent of His will? Whether it was Socrates or Plato who first formulated this dilemma, it is surely a good point.

In the *Alcibiades*, we are shown Socrates getting to work on someone at greater length. Though traditionally listed amongst Plato's works, scholars now question that attribution, if only because it is a good deal easier to interpret than those that are unquestionably his. (It seems that Plato, like Socrates, did not intend to give us ready-made doctrines, rather he wants us to think for ourselves, and he encourages us to do so by not telling us which voice in the dialogues represents his own view.) Alcibiades was a brilliant politician and military leader during the Peloponnesian War, but became notorious for his treachery when he defected to Sparta, and later served Persia. In this dialogue, he is represented as a beautiful, promising teenage boy of just the kind that Greek men fell in love with. (Even if we are not homophobic, we may find it difficult to understand ancient Greek society in which homosexual affairs were quite normal. Women and heterosexuality hardly get a mention!) Socrates' love for Alcibiades is represented as a chaste "Platonic" love that involves an educative relationship; his primary concern is for the state of Alcibiades' soul.

Most of this dialogue is self-explanatory, even a tad pedestrian. Alcibiades expresses his political ambition to "advise the Athenians" on policy in war and peace, but Socrates persuades him, by the hard grind of persistent questioning, that he doesn't know what he is talking about, and is in sore need of a proper education. We all need "self-cultivation" (124d), but self-knowledge is a difficult thing (129a), yet our primary task is to cultivate our souls (132c). And if the soul is to come to know itself, it must learn from another soul, one that contains wisdom, what it is that makes a soul good. The wise part of the soul resembles the divine, and someone who looks at that, and "grasps everything divine", will have the best grasp of himself as well (133b). It is impossible for anyone to prosper unless he is "self-controlled and good", so if Alcibiades is to fulfil his ambition to be a successful politician, he must not only be virtuous himself, but must "impart virtue to the citizens" (134c). If the historical Alcibiades really received any such moral lessons from Socrates, it seems he did not take them to heart!

To give the reader a taste of what Socratic dialogue is like, here is a brief sample passage of argument from *Alcibiades*, 129d:

SOCRATES. This is what I was just asking—doesn't the user of a thing always seem to be different from what he's using?

ALCIBIADES. It seems so.

SOCRATES. Let's think about the shoemaker again. Does he cut with his tools only, or does he also cut with his hands?

ALCIBIADES. With his hands, too.

SOCRATES. So he uses his hands, too.

ALCIBIADES. Yes.

SOCRATES. And doesn't he use his eyes, too, in the shoemaking?

ALCIBIADES. Yes.

SOCRATES. Didn't we agree that the person who uses something is different from the thing he uses?

ALCIBIADES. Yes.

SOCRATES. So the shoemaker and the lyre-player are different from the hands and eyes they use in their work.

ALCIBIADES. So it seems.

SOCRATES. Doesn't a man use his whole body, too?

ALCIBIADES. Certainly.

SOCRATES. And we agreed that the user is different from the thing being used.

ALCIBIADES. Yes.

SOCRATES. So a man is different from his body.

ALCIBIADES. So it seems.

SOCRATES. Then what is a man?

ALCIBIADES. I don't know what to say.

SOCRATES. Yes, you do — say that it's what uses the body.

ALCIBIADES. Yes.

SOCRATES. What else uses it but the soul?

ALCIBIADES. Nothing else.

SOCRATES. And doesn't the soul rule the body?

ALCIBIADES. Yes.

This is not the most stylish of passages (another reason why it is doubted whether Plato himself wrote it). Socrates' interlocutors are not always such putty in his hands: sometimes they resist, and things get more interesting! It may well induce a rabbit-out-of-hat suspicion when a weighty metaphysical conclusion about the distinction between body and soul is produced out of apparently trivial premises. But if we want to question the conclusion, the challenge is to pinpoint exactly where the argument goes wrong. As always with Socrates, we are made to think.

In the *Protagoras*, which has been described as the dramatic masterpiece among Plato's dialogues, Socrates engages in argument with the famous older sophist; and unusually, this is represented as a contest between intellectual equals (we can see this as Plato debating with himself — and inviting us to do the same). Protagoras claims to be able to teach virtue (318b), but Socrates objects that although many crafts and techniques are passed on by teaching, he does not see much evidence that virtue can be taught, for even the best citizens do not seem able to impart their virtues to their sons (319e). Protagoras replies with a creation story: "It is because humans had a share of the divine dispensation that they alone among animals worshipped the gods, with whom they had a kind of kinship" (322a) — which reminds us of the Biblical idea that man is made in the image of God. But, Protagoras continues, humans did not possess the art of politics, so to prevent them wiping themselves out in conflict, Zeus gave them a sense of shame and justice. So everyone has some innate sense of morality, but it needs education by praise and blame, punishment and reward (323c); thus children are taught and corrected from an early age, for "all of human life requires a high degree of rhythm and harmony" (326b).

At the end of Protagoras's long speech, Socrates professes himself deeply impressed, but says that there is just one small matter on which he needs further guidance. Of course it turns out to be a deep and difficult philosophical issue, namely whether "virtue" is really a single thing, with the conventional Greek virtues of wisdom, justice, temperance, piety, and courage as its *parts* (329d). Socrates gets Protagoras tangled up in knots over this question, so much so that the older man becomes annoyed and threatens to break off the discussion; the bystanders have to intervene with their own advice and suggestions. Eventually he consents to resume provided he can ask the questions, and he then engages Socrates in a protracted discussion of the morals to be learned from various Greek poems. In the midst of this digression, Socrates comes out with a very surprising statement:

> I am pretty sure that none of the wise men thinks that any human being willingly makes a mistake or willingly does anything wrong or bad. They know very well that anyone who does anything wrong or bad does so involuntarily. (*Protagoras* 345e)

Unusually here, we find Socrates coming out with a definite philosophical thesis of his own — and a rather counter-intuitive one at that.

Before we leave the *Protagoras*, it is worth quoting an extended comparison Socrates makes between ethics as the art of deciding which pleasures in life are really worth going for as opposed to those that are immediately available, and the art of measurement which decides which objects are really the largest:

> If then our well-being depended upon this, doing and choosing large things, avoiding and not doing the small ones, what would we see as our salvation in life? Would it be the art of measurement or the power of appearance? While the power of appearance often makes us wander all over the place in confusion, often changing our minds about the same things and regretting our actions and choices with respect to things large and small, the art of measurement in contrast, would make the appearances lose their power by showing us the truth, would give us peace of mind firmly rooted in the truth and would save our life. (*Protagoras* 356d)

This would not look out of place in the New Testament: St. Paul also emphasizes the need for wise self-control. Socrates uses this analogy with measurement to back up his already-mentioned thesis that "those who make mistakes with regard to the choice of pleasure and pain, in other words, with regard to good and bad, do so because of a lack of knowledge", i.e. they are ignorant of the true "measurement" of good and bad (357d).

The *Gorgias*, another subtle and lengthy dialogue, takes these ethical issues further. An important new theme is Socrates' striking thesis that it is better to suffer injustice than to do it (469b, 474b, 509c) — which can be compared to the "Beatitudes" in Jesus's "Sermon on the Mount", for example "Blessed are those who are persecuted in the cause of right; the Kingdom of Heaven is theirs" (*Matthew* 5:10). Corruption of one's own soul is the worst and most shameful thing of all (477e, 479b) — a thought also emphasized by Jesus. In the second half of the *Gorgias*, Socrates confronts the cynical view, put into the mouth of Callicles, that it is a law of nature that the "better" man, by which he means the more capable and stronger, should have a greater share of everything. In effect, Callicles is saying that might is right, and that ethical philosophizing is an unmanly thing; he even says at one point that "the man who'll live correctly ought to allow his own appetites to get as large as possible and not restrain them" (491e). There were people exemplifying this view in ancient Athens, and even more conspicuously in the Roman culture that followed — and there are plenty more today! In the *Gorgias* Socrates persuades Callicles that real happiness cannot be attained that way, and that self-discipline is necessary for individual happiness (505b), and that:

> partnerships and friendship, orderliness, self-control, and justice hold together heaven and earth, and gods and men, and that is why they call this universe a world-order. (*Gorgias* 508a)

A few comments on Socrates' philosophy

Although Socrates is represented in these dialogues as making a sharp contrast between body and soul, and as telling a story about the afterlife involving the separation of soul from body, this may well be Plato rather than the historical Socrates speaking. We know that Plato believed these things (see the *Phaedo*), but we cannot be sure that Socrates did. And it seems to me that in any case, the ethical message of the Socratic dialogues would not be substantially changed by substituting the word "mind" for "soul", and remaining neutral or sceptical about life after death.

Speaking for myself, I find Socrates' approach to philosophy and his main ethical message to be very impressive. Sometimes the nitty-gritty of the arguments in Plato's dialogues seems to go on too long, and to verge on mere verbal play. One can understand a comment that Wittgenstein penned in 1931:

> Reading the Socratic dialogues, one has the feeling: what a frightful waste of time! What's the point of these arguments that prove nothing and clarify nothing. (Ludwig Wittgenstein, *Culture and Value*, revised second edition, p. 21)

That is a very common reaction to philosophical discussion, which can indeed all-too-easily lose its grasp of any serious issue, and descend to the level of intellectual play, point-scoring, vanity—and sheer confusion! But it seems to me that this is a case of one great philosopher, perhaps on an off-day or in a dark mood, failing to understand two others (Socrates and Plato). Socrates' ethical seriousness and lack of vanity come through strongly in the *Apology*, and in the other dialogues Plato artfully represents Socrates (how far it is the historical Socrates does not matter very much) engaging in philosophical discussion which always has some serious interest behind it, being polite to his interlocutors even while disputing their views and arguments, being prepared to follow the argument where it leads, not being satisfied with inadequate answers, and not being ashamed to acknowledge ignorance, while not giving up hope of reaching better understanding. These seem to me to be intellectual virtues, but not merely that—they display *philo-sophia*, love of wisdom.

To be sure, it requires a patient and philosophically-inclined mind to follow the twist and turns of a typical Socratic dialogue all the way through (apart from the *Apology*, which is easier, but not trivial). The works of philosophers like Plato are unlikely to have the immediate spiritually-convincing power of the writings in the New Testament, especially the one-liners of Jesus and Paul. Plato's Socratic dialogues are in the different genre of philosophical argument, though there is literary artfulness in their construction. However there are some brief passages which vividly express the essence of what seems to have been Socrates' own thought (and I have quoted a few of them above).

Many people will find Socrates (and certainly Plato) over-intellectual. He tends to assume that to know what a given kind of thing is, one must be able to give an explicit verbal definition of it—for instance, to know what courage is, one must be able to define it in words. But surely someone who can reliably recognize instances of X can be said to know what X is, even if they can't come up with a watertight general definition. Moreover, Socrates is represented as thinking that to *be* courageous one must know what courage is in this definitional sense, and conversely that if one knows what courage is, one will be courageous. More generally, the thesis would be that to be virtuous, to be a good human being, it is both necessary and sufficient to *know* what human virtue is.

But that does not sound right—it seems to involve an intellectualizing fallacy. Surely one does not have to have the correct *theory* of virtue in order to *be* virtuous? Conversely, couldn't someone be right about the theory, yet still go wrong in practice? Don't we often fail to practise what we preach? As we have seen, Socrates seems to have been committed to the doctrine that nobody knowingly or willingly does what he or she thinks to be wrong. But this conflicts with the obvious facts about human nature: we often know quite well what we ought to do, and yet somehow or other we don't get around to doing it—indeed we sometimes find ourselves unwilling to do it.

But to voice such questions and criticisms is entirely in the spirit of the Socratic dialogues. The Socrates represented to us in these seminal works of human thought is someone committed to open-ended inquiry, who does not present us with doctrines to be believed on his authority, or on anyone else's. In this, there is a contrast with much religious practice, where we are typically expected to accept certain theological claims or ethical commandments because they are supposed to have the authority of divine revelation behind them. It is intriguing to imagine Jesus or St. Paul—or many advocates of various kinds of religion ever since—taking part in Socratic dialogue! Socrates invites us to *think*, not just to *believe*, and to join in an ongoing debate about what matters most in human life.

Further reading

If you would like to try reading some Socratic dialogues for yourself, I would suggest starting with those discussed above, namely the *Apology, Euthyphro, Alcibiades, Protagoras* and *Gorgias*. If you can get through these, you'll be ready for the rest! In references and quotations above, I have used the standard numbering system for the pages of Plato's texts.

My quotations are from the translations in *Plato: Complete Works*, edited by John M. Cooper (Indianapolis: Hackett 1997). (There are many other translations and editions of Plato's dialogues.)

There is a good introduction to *Socrates* by Christopher Taylor in the Oxford University Press Very Short Introduction series (2000).

For a scholarly treatment of Socrates, see *The Philosophy of Socrates*, by Thomas C. Brickhouse and Nicholas D. Smith (Boulder: Westview 2000).

CHAPTER 3
THE TEACHING OF JESUS

Ancient Jewish history up to the time of Jesus

The Jews have maintained their religious and ethnic identity through many trials and tribulations over at least three millennia. Judaism as it exists today has grown out of the Rabbinic tradition that developed after the birth of Christianity, and in reaction to it (as we will see in Chapter 5). But Jesus (whatever else he is claimed to be) was a Jewish prophetic teacher of the early 1st century, so to understand him we need to know something of the *ancient* Jewish tradition from which he sprang.

The Hebrew scriptures (which Christians call the Old Testament) are a mixed collection of very different kinds of writing—creation stories, stories of God's dealing with significant individuals, histories, prayers, proverbs, theology, prophecy, etc.—compiled over a period of at least a thousand years, from about 1200 to 200 BCE. The first eleven chapters of *Genesis*, the opening book, tell a story of the creation of *all* mankind (including the flood, and the restoration after it), but all the rest of the Hebrew Bible tells the story of one people, "the children of Israel", who thought of themselves as specially chosen by God through their ancestor Abraham. They migrated into Egypt, and were enslaved by the pharaohs. Then God called Moses to lead "His chosen people" out of bondage in Egypt, as described in *Exodus* (historians date these events to about 1300 BCE). After Moses' death, Joshua led them in a conquest of "the Promised Land" of Canaan, which involved the (supposedly God-commanded) genocide of its previous inhabitants, as was the fashion of the time (see *Joshua* 6:21, 8:24, 9:27, *Judges* 1:8, 11:33). The Jews then regarded this territory (present-day Israel and Palestine) as given to them by God (and some Jews maintain this even now).

Once the promised land had been settled, Israelite society grew and began to prosper. The Jewish religion with "Yahweh" as its single transcendent God was sharply different from Egypt's cult of divine pharaohs, and from Canaanite worship of the dying and rising fertility god Baal. The separate identity of "the children of Israel" was maintained by the circumcision of male infants, the observance of the Sabbath, and the elaborate dietary restrictions laid down in the "Torah", the first five books of the Hebrew Bible. A centralized nation emerged later, with Jerusalem as its capital. The monarchy started uncertainly with Saul, but David succeeded him as undisputed king. In the reign of David's son Solomon (around 1000 BCE) the Jewish nation enjoyed unprecedented peace and prosperity, and the first great temple in Jerusalem was completed.

After Solomon's death, however, there was a split into two separate kingdoms: Judah, centred on Jerusalem, and Israel in the north, centred on Samaria. These small states were vulnerable to neighbouring empires: Egypt on one side and Assyria, then Babylon, then Persia on the other. Under kings of varying quality, the two Jewish states maintained a precarious independence until 722 BCE, when the advancing Assyrians overran Israel, as had been foreseen by some of the prophets who interpreted these events as God's punishment for the sins of the Israelites. Assyria itself soon fell to the Babylonians, who also conquered Judah, taking Jerusalem in 587 BCE as prophesied by *Jeremiah* 19:1-11. The temple was sacked, and most of the inhabitants were deported to Babylon (whose ruins now lie in the sands in present-day Iraq).

The Babylonian exile was the first great disruption of Jewish existence since the deliverance from Egypt. Up to then, "Yahweh" had been seen as the national god of Israel, a rival to other tribal gods such as Baal. But defeat and exile forced the Jews to live in dispersion as minorities in other cultures (as they have done from 70-1948 CE). Some of them came to believe that their religion was not dependent on a Jewish national state, and they began to think of God as transcending national boundaries. Babylon fell to Persia under Cyrus the great, and his empire brought peace and allowed religious diversity in its territories. Jews then had to decide how far to assimilate to the cultures in which they were living—and on that they differed sharply amongst themselves (as they have done right down to the present day). Cyrus allowed the descendants of the exiled people of Judah to return to Jerusalem, where they constructed the "Second Temple".

In this period, the status of the inhabitants of Samaria (the area of the former northern Jewish kingdom) became controversial. The Assyrians had planted in peoples from other lands, and though there remained some of Jewish descent, the Samaritans (as they came to be called) departed from the strict traditions laid down in the Torah (2 Kings 17:24-33). So the Jews returning from the Babylonian exile regarded them as unorthodox, and would not allow them to take part in the rebuilding of the temple (Ezra 4:2-3). The Samaritans developed their own traditions based on Mount Gerizim instead of the Temple, and they maintained a separate quasi-Jewish identity that lasted into Jesus's day, and even up to modern times.

But once again the Near East was subject to world-historical changes. About 400 BCE the Persian empire fell to the armies of Alexander the Great, and Greek language, culture and thought spread around the region. Again Jews had to decide how far to assimilate to a new culture, and again they reached different decisions. The Jewish scriptures were translated into Greek. Some writings such as *The Wisdom of Solomon* (in the Old Testament Apocrypha) seem designed to reconcile Jewish and Greek thought. In that book, wisdom is personified, almost deified, and in female gender (7:25-27). The idea of a life after death entered Jewish thought around this time, conceived as bodily resurrection rather than survival of a disembodied soul (Daniel 12:3). But belief in resurrection did not become universal, and the Sadducees (one of various Jewish parties with rival theologies) did not accept it.

Again the Jews suffered grievously under the Hellenistic successors of Alexander's empire. In the 2nd century BCE Antiochus IV tried to eradicate Judaism and replace it by Greek religion and culture. When the Jews resisted, he slaughtered thousands of them and looted the Temple. Circumcision and possession of the Book of the Law were punished by death. But many Jews resisted, and Judas (called Maccabeus) led a successful revolt, recaptured Jerusalem, and cleansed the Temple. The victorious Maccabees then persecuted those Jews who had compromised with Hellenism.

In these times of exile, conquest and persecution, there arose longings for national redemption and a restoration of the throne of David—and the distinction between political and spiritual renewal was never very clear. The prophets talked of God's anger and His punishment of the Israelites for their unfaithfulness to Him, but they also spoke of His merciful forgiveness, and His future regeneration of the people of Israel and even the whole of creation. The authors of the composite book of Isaiah use ecstatic language to express this vision of God's forgiveness, redemption, and new creation: "Then will the glory of the Lord be revealed, and all mankind will see it" (*Isaiah* 40:5); 'See, I am creating new heavens and a new earth!' (65:17). The prophetic hope arose for a divinely-appointed saviour, sometimes called 'the Messiah'. *Isaiah* 9:6–7 (unforgettably set to music by Handel) says 'Unto us a child is born', whose titles will be 'Wonderful Counsellor, Mighty Hero, Eternal Father, and Prince of Peace'.

In the book of Daniel, which dates from the early 2nd century BCE, there are apocalyptic visions apparently referring to the powerful empires that had dominated Israel's existence, and there appears a mysterious figure who is predicted to bring a divine fulfillment history:

> I saw one like a human being [*the Hebrew phrase was traditionally translated as "Son of Man"*] coming with the clouds of heaven; he approached the Ancient in Years [i.e. God] and was presented to him. Sovereignty and glory and kingly power were given to him, so that all peoples and nations of every language should serve him; his sovereignty was to be an everlasting kingdom which was not to pass away, and his kingly power was never to be destroyed (*Daniel* 7:13–14).

Such Messianic hopes and expectations — whether in political or supernatural form, or a mixture of the two — were very much around in Jesus's time, and they have recurred in later Judaism (usually to be disappointed).

The independence won by the Maccabees was short-lived, for the Romans were now on the rise, and in 63 BCE they conquered Palestine, ruling it through "procurators" such as Pontius Pilate and allies such as King Herod. The Jewish religious authorities — the Sanhedrin, chief priests and scribes mentioned in the gospels — had to accept Roman political authority if they were to maintain their religious jurisdiction. So they were caught between the demands of the Romans to maintain order and taxation, and the continuing aspirations of their own people for a restored Jewish state. As before and since, there were deep divisions within Judaism. In the time of Jesus there were the Pharisees and the Sadducees mentioned in the gospels, but also the Essenes, a radical monastic sect who produced the recently-discovered Dead Sea Scrolls.

Just one generation after Jesus revolt against Roman rule broke out, led by the Zealots, the violently revolutionary Jewish party. They briefly gained control of Jerusalem, but it was always going to be an unequal contest, and in 70 CE the Romans retook the city and utterly destroyed the second temple (as Jesus is represented as foreseeing at *Mark* 13:2). The remaining Zealots retreated to the hilltop fortress of Masada, where they committed suicide rather than surrender. From that date until 1948 there was no Jewish state, and the Jews existed in dispersion across many lands, often as a persecuted minority.

The sources of our knowledge of Jesus

There are enough references by ancient writers apart from the New Testament for us to be assured beyond all reasonable doubt that there was indeed a 1st-century Jewish religious teacher known as Jesus of Nazareth, who gained some popular following but was crucified on the orders of Pontius Pilate in about 30 CE. But anything else that people claim about him is not universally agreed—to put it mildly!

Jesus did not leave any writings of his own, but he exerted a magnetic personal influence on his disciples and many others who met him, and he has had an enormous world-historical influence down the centuries ever since through the writings and preaching of his followers. The texts in the Christian New Testament are our major source for knowledge of Jesus, but it has to be acknowledged straight away that they are not neutral historical records. They are devotional and inspirational writings designed to convince people not merely of the validity of Jesus's teaching, but of the cosmic significance of his life and death and alleged resurrection, which his followers claimed show him to be uniquely divine.

The earliest Christian documents were the letters ("epistles") written by Paul and other apostles to the early Christian communities, most of which (both epistles and communities) are now thought to predate the gospels. Paul's first letter to the *Thessalonians* is thought to have been written about 51 CE, only twenty years after the crucifixion. His longest and theologically most weighty letters, addressed to the *Romans* and *Corinthians*, were probably composed in the same decade.

The four gospel narratives of Jesus's life are intriguingly different from each other. Mark's gospel, the shortest and probably the earliest, is a collection of stories and traditions about Jesus assembled around 70 CE. It begins with John the Baptist preaching in the wilderness, when the adult Jesus arrives for baptism, and a voice from heaven says "You are my beloved Son" (*Mark* 1:11). It takes us through Jesus' ministry in Galilee proclaiming that "the kingdom of God is at hand", healing and miracle-working. Mark gives special emphasis to Jesus's casting out of "evil spirits" or demons, and rather less to his teaching in parables. At a central point Jesus asks his disciples who they think he is, and Peter replies "You are the Messiah" (8:29). Jesus does not deny this, but mysteriously tells them to keep it secret. There follows the "transfiguration" scene on a mountain-top, where Moses and Elijah appear from the distant past to talk with Jesus amidst an unearthly light (9:2-4). Conflict with the Jewish authorities grows, and soon after entering Jerusalem Jesus is arrested, questioned by the Jewish high priests and the Roman governor Pilate, and sent for crucifixion.

The gospels of *Matthew* and *Luke* repeat much of the material in *Mark*; they overlap in other ways, and each contains some features of its own. Scholars conclude that Matthew and Luke had access to *Mark*, and to another independent source long since lost. *Matthew* has been described as the most Jewish of the gospels: it starts with an elaborate genealogy purporting to show that Jesus was descended by fourteen generations from King David, and by fourteen more back to Abraham. But it also says that Mary miraculously conceived him while remaining a virgin, in fulfillment of an Old Testament prophecy (1:18-25), and if so, Joseph was not Jesus's biological father. Matthew organizes Jesus's teaching into five long discourses, starting with what is known as "the Sermon on the Mount" (Ch. 5-7). There is a strong emphasis that the Jewish laws remain in full force (5:17-19).

The gospel of *Luke* was authored by a Gentile (i.e. non-Jewish) Christian; like the others, it was written in Greek, but it has a more literary style, including a formal preface. Luke gives by far the most detailed account of Jesus's birth and infancy, including the beloved Christmas stories and some beautiful poems (the *"Magnificat"*, *"Benedictus"*, and *"Nunc Dimittis"*) which have been incorporated into many liturgies. There is an intriguing glimpse of the adolescent Jesus evading his parents to stay behind in the temple at Jerusalem, and surprising the rabbis by the intelligence of his questions (2:41-52). (As with all these stories, how much is based on eyewitness testimony, probable inference, or pious invention, it is impossible to tell.) Luke went on to write a second volume, entitled *The Acts of the Apostles*, which tells the story of the first Christians and their missionary achievements. Despite their differences of emphasis Matthew, Mark and Luke offer a very similar overall account of Jesus's life and death, so they are known as the "synoptic" gospels, i.e. they can be put together to make up a common view of Jesus's life and teaching.

John's gospel seems to come from an independent tradition, which may go back to John the son of Zebedee, one of Jesus's disciples. It is thought to be the latest, dating from about 100 CE, and offers a somewhat different chronology of Jesus's ministry, putting the cleansing of the temple at the beginning (it and the synoptics cannot both be historically correct). More importantly, from the very start John is more thoroughly impregnated with theological interpretation. In the famous cosmic prologue, Jesus is identified with "the Word" (*logos*) that was with God in the beginning, at the creation of the world (there is an influence from Greek philosophy here). Then the human Jesus is suddenly introduced, calling disciples to follow him, with some curiously irrelevant details that have the flavour of someone's memory of an actual scene. We are told of this happening "about the tenth hour", and of Nathaniel, when informed by Philip that the Messiah is here and he is Jesus of Nazareth, exclaiming "Nazareth! Can anything good come from Nazareth?" And Jesus is said to have "seen" Nathaniel under a fig tree before arriving on the scene (*John* 1:35-51). Here is the meaning of life, history and the universe being revealed, at four o'clock one afternoon, under a fig tree, by someone of dubious origin, in provincial Galilee! It seems the writer wants to persuade us that in the midst of very ordinary life, something truly extraordinary can happen.

John contains many other stories of Jesus's conversations and healings that may have been based on actual memories, but have been artfully constructed into a series of seven "signs", i.e. miracles that are supposed not only to demonstrate supernatural power, but to convince us of spiritual truths. A striking feature of *John* is the lengthy discourses that are put into the mouth of Jesus, in which he ascribes to himself cosmic significance (3:16), unique saving power (6:44), and unity with God the Father (5:18, 8:58, 10:30). We cannot possibly know how much, if any, of this is based on what Jesus actually said (it beggars belief that anyone present could have remembered it all, especially in the absence of tape-recorders or shorthand notebooks!). These discourses involve the incarnational theology—the claim that Jesus was not merely a divinely-appointed man, but God himself in human form—that some of the early Christians had arrived at, especially Paul, who wrote that Jesus "was in the form of God; yet he laid no claim to equality with God, but made himself nothing, assuming the form of a slave" (*Philippians* 2:6-7). Another peculiarity of *John* is the increasingly sharp conflict between Jesus and "the Jews", even though Jesus himself was a Jew! Presumably this reflects the hostile separation that had emerged between Christians (who had initially been a sect within Judaism) and mainstream Judaism. Unfortunately these passages have given encouragement to recurring anti-semitism down the centuries ever since.

As well as the canonical epistles and gospels there are various "apocryphal" writings from the early Christian centuries that were not admitted into the "canon" of the New Testament. Some of them were not rediscovered until a jar of ancient texts turned up in the sands of Egypt in 1945 (presumably they were hidden away when orders came through from the then-dominant church hierarchy to burn all the non-canonical gospels). It has taken time for scholars to preserve, decipher and interpret these intriguing fragments, and whether any of them tell us anything new about Jesus himself is a matter of historical and theological controversy. Knowledge of them has hardly penetrated beyond the academic journal and seminar into the pew, the pulpit or the newspaper, but Elaine Pagels has provided a very readable account. She argues that there was intense rivalry and controversy between different groups of followers of Jesus in the 1st century, and that the gospel of John was written in conscious opposition to other accounts of Jesus's life and teaching, such as the *Gospel of Thomas*. *John* emphasizes from the start that Jesus was not merely a divinely-inspired or divinely-appointed "Messiah", "son of man" or "son of God" (for all those traditional Jewish titles can be interpreted that way) but that he was (and is) the eternal Creator, God Himself incarnated in human flesh—a claim which was totally foreign, and indeed blasphemous, to the Jews.

The *Gospel of Thomas* has now been published in translation: it has no narrative of events, only a list of Jesus's teaching in the form of parables and short enigmatic sayings. Some of these are versions of what we already know from the canonical gospels (which does something to reassure us that they have a common source in Jesus himself), while others are obscure in meaning, highly metaphorical, and suggest that the reader (or hearer) is supposed to "intuit" a hidden spiritual meaning for himself or herself. I will refer to it below.

Since the nineteenth century there have been many attempts to "get behind" the theologically-committed representations in the canonical gospels, to unearth "the real historical facts" about Jesus. But it has been generally recognized that this "quest for the historical Jesus" inevitably fails: the "facts" a writer comes up with will always be infected by his or her own preconceptions. There can be no such thing as a neutral, "objective", merely historical, account of the life and teaching of Jesus, and I do not pretend to offer one here.

In what follows I propose to concentrate on his teaching, mostly from the three synoptic gospels. Though I find most of it impressive, some of it is puzzling, and I do not feel obliged to accept everything just because he is reported to have said it. I will not discuss the miracles attributed to him, except to say that there is no need to deny that he may have been a very effective faith healer (after all, the phenomenon is well-known). In John various cosmic claims are put into Jesus's mouth: he claims to be the Messiah (4:25-26), the Son of God (5:16-47), the bread which comes down from heaven (6:30-58), and to have existed before Abraham was born (8:58). But scholars have long debated how Jesus thought of himself without coming up with a consensus answer. I leave the thoroughly controversial matters of Jesus's alleged divinity and resurrection for Chapters 5 and 10.

There are some striking parallels between our knowledge of Jesus and of Socrates. In both cases, we know of the original person only through the writings of others, and for the most important topics we have to rely on writers who had their own philosophical or religious agendas—Plato in Socrates' case, the four evangelists for Jesus. But there are big differences too: there are no reports of Socrates performing miracles or being resurrected, nor was he treated by his followers as the incarnation of God. He came from a different cultural background in which there was no Messianic expectation, no belief in a personal God who could intervene in history.

Jesus's teaching

There is quite a variety of teaching to be found in the gospels, so it is tempting to "cherry-pick" the bits we like, and pass over the rest. We can find on one hand the "gentle Jesus, meek and mild" of Victorian hymnody, who encouraged children to approach him, and said that "the Kingdom of Heaven belongs to such as these" (*Matthew* 18:1-5, 19:13-15). But on the other hand, there are threats of divisiveness and of hell-fire, and there is the apparently unedifying story of the hungry Jesus cursing a fig tree that did not have any fruit, when it was the wrong season for fruit, anyway! (*Mark* 11:12-14, 20-22). It is difficult to see why *that* little story was thought fit to include in a gospel, except perhaps to see the withering of the tree as a proof of Jesus's supernatural power—but it still seems a rather bad-tempered use of power (who would punish a *tree*?). I will try to offer a representative sample of Jesus's teaching, with some comments that will inevitably be controversial.

At the beginning of his ministry Jesus seems to have proclaimed the coming of "the Kingdom of God" (*Mark* 1:15)—also called "the Kingdom of Heaven" (*Matthew* 4:17). But what do these phrases mean: a political event within history such as a renewed Jewish kingship, a divinely-wrought end to all human history, or a purely spiritual change within individuals? Apparently this was not clear to Jesus's hearers either. Some saw him as a new Jewish national leader who would end the Roman occupation, others as the divinely-appointed Messiah or "Son of Man" who would establish God's kingdom for ever. He was manifestly a healer, someone who brought both physical and spiritual healing to people. Perhaps some saw him as combining all *three* roles, but that is not an option for us now—not the bit about expelling the Romans and re-establishing a Jewish kingship, anyway; and perhaps we can accept the spiritual interpretation without the eschatological one.

Jesus's conception of "the Kingdom of God" has *at least* the spiritual meaning, since so many of his parables suggest some such elucidation of the phrase. In the parable of the sower, the seed is said to represent "the word"—i.e. the word of God, or the divinely-given potential in all of us—and the fate of different seeds represents the different degrees of spiritual growth, or failure to grow, in various people (*Mark* 4:3–20; *Matthew* 13:4–23). Jesus's comparisons of the Kingdom of God to the tiny mustard seed that grows into a substantial tree, and to the yeast that makes the bread rise, also suggest the potentially enormous consequences of inner spiritual change, or lack of it (*Matthew* 13:31–33; *Luke* 13:18–21). Many of the parables are ambiguous enough to allow eschatological interpretations as well, but Luke has a saying that strongly indicates a purely spiritual meaning:

> The Pharisees asked him, "When will the kingdom of God come?" He answered, "You cannot tell by observation when the kingdom of God comes. You cannot say, 'Look, here it is!' or 'There it is!' For the kingdom of God is among you!" (*Luke* 17:20–21)

In the *Gospel of Thomas*, the "Kingdom" theme recurs, with some interesting variations, almost entirely on the spiritual side. Here is "logion" (or saying) 3:

> Jesus said:

THE TEACHING OF JESUS

> If those who guide your Being say to you:
> "Behold the Kingdom is in the heaven,"
> then the birds of the sky will precede you;
> if they say to you: "It is in the sea," then the fish will precede you.
> But the Kingdom is in your centre
> and is about you.
> When you Know your Selves
> then you will be Known,
> and you will be aware that you are
> the sons of the Living father.
> But if you do not Know yourselves
> then you are in poverty,
> and you are the poverty.

The reference to self-knowledge here picks up on a Socratic theme (presumably unintentionally). But lest you run away with the impression of a fashionably existentialist or new-age Jesus, read logion 57 which sounds as eschatological as anything in the canonical New Testament. Even here, however, a spiritual interpretation is possible, that the "weeds" are the products of evil tendencies in human nature, which need to be eradicated:

> Jesus said:
> The Kingdom of the Father is like a man
> who owned good seed.
> His enemy came by night,
> he sowed weeds among the good seed.
> The man did not allow the labourers to pull up the weeds;
> he said to them: lest perhaps you should go,
> saying, "we will pull up the weeds,"
> and you pull up the wheat with it.
> For on the day of the harvest
> the seeds will appear;
> they will be pulled up and will be burned.

I will come to hell-fire below (and I am aware of the double meaning in that!), but love is surely a more fundamental aspect of Jesus's teaching. His famous theme of love of God and love of neighbour is not original to him, for it is already found in the Torah. When challenged by one of the scribes to say which is the greatest of all the commandments, Jesus replied:

> The first is "Hear, O Israel, the Lord our God is the one Lord, and you must love the Lord your God with all your heart, with all your soul, with all your mind, and with all your strength". The second is this: "You must love your neighbour as yourself". No other commandment is greater than these. (*Mark* 12:29-31; see also *Matthew* 22:37-40 and *Luke* 10:27)

These words are quoted from *Deuteronomy* 6:4-5 and *Leviticus* 19:18, where they are rather buried amid a host of much less appealing Jewish regulations. Jesus was obviously steeped in the scriptures, but he brought a deeper and more challenging interpretation to the idea of loving one's neighbour. The well-known story of the good Samaritan (*Luke* 10:29-37) is told by Jesus in response to the question "Who is my neighbour?" and his point is that it includes anyone one meets (though oddly, it is the helper rather than the victim who is so described in the story).

Jesus extends the imperative of love still further when he says "Love your enemies and pray for your persecutors" (*Matthew* 5:44). Indeed he takes it to what may seem a quite impractical extreme:

> Love your enemies; do good to them that hate you; bless those who curse you; pray for those whose treat you spitefully. If anyone hits you on the cheek, offer the other also; if anyone takes your coat, let him have your shirt as well. Give to anyone who asks you; if anyone takes what is yours, do not demand it back. (*Luke* 6:27-30)

A natural reaction is to say "Beautiful—but impossible! How could anyone survive by practising such an utterly selfless ethic? How could human society continue on such a basis? Surely this would allow the unscrupulous and wicked to walk all over the rest of us?" To interpret Jesus anything other than literally may risk missing the truly radical demands of his teaching, but perhaps we can see behind these words a Jewish version of Socrates' similarly counter-intuitive doctrine that it is better to suffer injustice than to do it. However there also seems to be a thought which may go further, namely that even if we cannot "love" our enemies in the ordinary sense we should strive not to be overwhelmed by the usual human reactions of anger, resentment, and vengefulness, but try to see wrongdoers as fallible human beings ("children of God") like ourselves, with their own pressures, needs and desires.

Another aspect of love is forgiveness. Love is easy when all is sweetness and light; forgiveness is what love needs when the going gets hard. Jesus says that we have to be prepared to forgive others, if we want to be forgiven by God (*Matthew* 6:12-15, 18:35; *Mark* 11:25). When asked how often we are to forgive someone who goes on wronging us, he says not just seven times, but seventy times seven (*Matthew* 18:21-22) — and I suppose he does not mean us to stop at 490! Again, this seems quite impossibly demanding; but at *Luke* 17:3-4 there is a modified version in which Jesus says "If your brother does wrong, reprove him; and if he repents, forgive him", and do this seven times a day, if necessary. Here forgiveness is made conditional on repentance — but presumably the *readiness* to forgive must always be there. Once again, there are no precise rules to be derived from what Jesus says, only an infinitely demanding ideal to inspire us, however difficult we find it to live up to.

Jesus's words "Give to anyone who asks you; if anyone takes what is yours, do not demand it back" might be toned down to mean that we should be ready for *occasional* acts of extraordinary generosity. I think we have to recognize that his style of teaching often involves extreme hyperbole, as shown in his sayings that we must attend to the plank in our own eye rather than fuss about the speck in someone else's (*Luke* 6:41-43), that if your right eye offends you, you should pluck it out (*Matthew* 5:29), that if anyone wants to become a disciple, he must hate his own mother and father, wife and children, brothers and sisters, even his own life (*Luke* 14:26). The imagery of these sayings is so hideous that we surely have to take them as using gross exaggeration to shock us out of our conventional thinking, making a spiritual point with an unforgettable phrase, however crude. A sober paraphrase might be that we should pay more attention to our own faults than to those of other people, and that anything which gets in the way of our devotion to God (or our highest ideals) may have to be sacrificed — even, in the most extreme situations, family relationships or life itself. Jesus provides an example himself, in his somewhat brusque dismissal of the claims of his own family (*Mark* 3:31-35), and of course in risking and facing death at the hands of the Jewish and Roman authorities of his time.

Hyperbole is also shown in Jesus's questioning of conventional notions of prudence:

> Think of the lilies, they neither spin nor weave: yet I tell you, Solomon in all his splendour was not attired like one of them. If that is how God clothes the grass, which is growing in the field today, and tomorrow is thrown on the stove, how much more will he clothe you! How little faith

you have! Do not set your minds on what you are to eat or drink; do not be anxious. These are all things that occupy the minds of the Gentiles, but your Father knows that you need them. No, set your minds on his kingdom, and the rest will be added to you. (*Luke* 12:27-31; *Matthew* 6:25-34)

Yet Jesus himself is elsewhere shown sending his disciples to buy food (*John* 4:8), getting concerned about the hunger of the crowds who had been following him (*Mark* 8:1-3), and as having made arrangements in advance for a colt to ride on in his fateful entry into Jerusalem (*Mark* 11:1-6). So we can hardly interpret him as saying that we should *never* take *any* "thought for the morrow", but rather that prudential anxieties should not be allowed to dominate everything else; that above and beyond our natural concerns for the continuation and comfort of our lives, we must always have some conception of what life is *for*. In the terminology of Chapter 1, we must always have some ideals, some things we love for their own sake. Jesus's teaching vividly expresses a spirit in which to live, but he does usually not give guidance for particular situations or lay down explicit rules.

There is hyperbole too in Jesus's response to the rich man who asked him "What must I do to win eternal life?" Over and above keeping the commandments, Jesus's answer is "Go, sell everything you have, and give to the poor, and you will have riches in heaven; and come, follow me" (*Mark* 10:17-22). (Those with an eagle eye for the texts may notice that at *Matthew* 19:21 and *Luke* 12:33 the injunction is to "sell your possessions", without using the word "all" or "everything".) But of course, if one sells literally *everything* one has, and gives all the proceeds to the poor, one will thereby become one of the poor oneself, and dependent on the handouts of others. When Mrs. Thatcher said in her "Sermon on the Mound" (to the Church of Scotland assembly in Edinburgh) that the good Samaritan needed to have financial resources to be able to help the victim of robbery, she had a point, even if she was twisting the story to fit her own political agenda. Those who take a vocation of poverty on joining a religious order give up personal possessions, but the religious institution then takes responsibility for their essential needs, so they do not have to *worry* ever again about food and clothing, housing or investments (unless they become abbot or abbess, and have to make decisions about such things on behalf of the whole community). Again, one has to presume (with some trepidation) that Jesus's words are not to be taken literally, that his point is to avoid over-attachment to possessions, since other things in life are more important. "Where your treasure is, there will your heart be also" (*Luke* 12:34). But again it is left to us to decide what counts as *over*-attachment.

What then is the relationship between Jesus's teaching and the Jewish tradition in which he was brought up? For Jews "the Law" meant not just the Ten Commandments, but the myriad rules and regulations governing agriculture, animal husbandry, cooking, cleansing, clothing, sexual relations, crime and punishment, the keeping of the Sabbath, the rituals of sacrifice, etc., set out at great length in the Torah. In Jesus's time, rival schools of thought had grown up amongst the rabbis about how to interpret and apply these rules. For example they disagreed about what counts as work, and therefore as prohibited on the Sabbath (and they still do!). But the whole spirit of Jesus's teaching transcends such legalism about details ("rule-worship"); he says as much when he accuses the Pharisees and scribes, with their fussing about rules of purification, of "setting aside the commandments of God in order to maintain the tradition of men" (*Mark* 7:1–23).

On the other hand, he is reported as saying that "So long as heaven and earth endure, not a letter, not a dot, will disappear from the law until all that must happen has happened" (*Matthew* 5:18; *Luke* 16:17). Yet he follows that up with a series of six sayings of the form "You have heard that our forefathers were told ... but what I tell you is this ..." — which suggests an extraordinary confidence in his own authority to amend or transcend the written laws that were (and are) so sacrosanct to Jewish traditionalists. The best remembered of these sayings is: "You have heard that they were told 'Do not commit adultery'. But what I tell you is this: If a man looks at a woman with a lustful eye, he has already committed adultery with her in his heart" (*Matthew* 5:27–28). (Jimmy Carter publicly applied it to himself, but it applies to all heterosexual males!) Jesus does not deny the validity of the original law, but he extends it to apply to the inner mental attitudes as well as the outward actions. Perhaps we can have some control over our own thoughts, but it is hard to believe that feeling tempted is every bit as bad as giving in to temptation.

On some occasions Jesus takes it on himself to break some of the traditional Jewish rules. He says that his disciples do not need to keep a fast that others were observing (*Mark* 2:19). When accused by the Pharisees of breaking the Sabbath by plucking ears of corn or performing healings, he engages in some arguments expounding scripture, but then he says that the Son of Man (by implication, himself) is Lord of the Sabbath (*Mark* 2:28; *Matthew* 12:8). He also declares that the Sabbath is made for man, not man for the Sabbath (*Mark* 2:28). That surely implies that Jews, or anyone else, do not need to get bogged down in litigious debates about what exactly counts as "work", which is to miss the point of the Sabbath — to keep one day of the week for lifting our eyes above *earning* a living to the *point* of living (something which modern secular society has increasingly erased). Jesus's critics amongst the Jewish religious authorities try to engage him in argument on tricky questions, with the aim (we are told) of catching him out. These passages are the nearest we get to Socratic dialogue, but the rules of engagement are very different, with scriptural passages playing the role of trumps — though subject to interpretation. Jesus sometimes plays that game, but he tends to leave it behind and come out with authoritative pronouncements of his own.

On the question of adultery and divorce, Jesus gives somewhat ambiguous answers in *Matthew* 19:3-9. When the Pharisees ask him about whether a man can divorce his wife for any cause he pleases, Jesus quotes *Genesis* 2:24, that man and wife "become one flesh", therefore "what God has joined together, man must not separate". The Pharisees point out that Moses laid down that a man who "finds something offensive" in his wife may divorce her by a certificate of dismissal (*Deuteronomy* 24:1). Jesus then transforms the debate, with what must have sounded to Jews like supreme arrogance, asserting on his own authority that what Moses said was only a concession to human weakness, and implying that the original ban on divorce remains in full force. But then he says, confusingly, that if a man divorces his wife for any reason *other than unchastity* and marries another, he commits adultery — which suggests an exception to the absolute ban on divorce he previously implied. (The version at *Mark* 10:11-12 is more consistent, for it does not contain the italicized clause.) Jesus clearly puts a very high value on marriage, seeing it as a divinely-appointed institution and each particular marriage as a divinely-approved fact, but he leaves us no clear instruction on how we are to cope with the ever-recurring situations in which people fall short of the highest ideals.

Also relevant here is the story of the woman taken in adultery at *John* 9:1-11. Once again, the scribes and Pharisees pose a difficult question, this time about a woman caught in the very act. (Surely they would catch the man too? — but the old double standard seems to be at work.) They challenge Jesus: "The law of Moses prescribes that she should be stoned. What do you say?" He bends down and writes in the sand, as if playing for time while he considers what to say, then he comes out with the famous words: "Let he among you who is without sin cast the first stone" — and one by one, they slink away. When they have all gone, he says to the woman "Go, and sin no more." The story is characteristic of Jesus, diverting attention from traditional and legalistic questions to the real source of our actions in the motivations of our hearts.

This leads us to note the very inclusive nature of Jesus's ministry. Early on, he was criticized for eating with "tax collectors and sinners" (*Mark* 2:15-17) — a phrase guaranteed to bring a smile to the face of those who have dealings with the Inland Revenue! The point in 1st-century Palestine was that tax collectors were collaborators with the hated Roman occupation (and no doubt had opportunities to keep a slice for themselves). Jesus's reply to reproaches about the company he kept was "It is not the healthy who need a doctor, but the sick; I did not come to call the virtuous, but sinners." He was even accused of being a glutton and a drunkard himself! *Luke* 7:36-50 tells the beautiful story of Jesus being invited to dinner at a Pharisee's house, and a woman of ill repute (presumably a prostitute) comes in and anoints his feet with myrrh, kissing them and wiping them with her tears. The Pharisee thinks to himself that if Jesus were a real prophet he would realize what a bad woman she is; but Jesus guesses his host's thoughts, and says that her great love proves that her sins have been forgiven.

Most of the people Jesus met were Jews, but there are some significant encounters with others. In *Mark* 7: 24-30 he travels into the territory of Tyre, a Gentile region, where he is implored by a Phoenician woman to heal her daughter. His first response seems unhelpful, even racist: "Let the children be satisfied first: it is not right to take the children's bread and throw it to the dogs" — meaning that the Jews have priority for healing, even in the most urgent cases (this is explicit in the version at *Matthew* 15:24). But the persistent Gentile mother replies: "Sir, even the dogs under the table eat the children's scraps". Then Jesus says: "For saying that, go, and you will find that the demon has left your daughter." The story as it stands is hardly edifying: it leaves us with the impression that Jesus would only perform healing for a Gentile because she comes up with a suitably clever reply, which conceded the validity of the implied discrimination. However, it is also possible to interpret the reported words as humorous bantering on both sides, referring to but not endorsing the existing discriminations.

Fortunately, there are more positive examples of Jesus's attitude to Gentiles. There is the story of his healing the Roman centurion's servant, and his commending the centurion for his faith (*Matthew* 8:5-13). And there are several intriguing dealings with Samaritans (whose tangled history I summarized in the introductory section above). Some references are not encouraging: Matthew has Jesus instructing his disciples not to go to Gentile or Samaritan areas, but to concentrate on "the lost sheep of the house of Israel" (*Matthew* 10:5-6), though this might have been a matter of short-term priority, i.e. preach to the Jews first, and to the rest later. Luke tells the story of the good Samaritan who helps an injured victim, after a Jewish priest and a Levite have passed by on the other side (*Luke* 10:30-37) — and ever since, we have connected Samaritans with *goodness*. And better still, there is Jesus's fascinating encounter with the Samaritan woman at Jacob's well in Samaria (*John* 4:4-42). As usual in John's gospel, the story is rich in allusion and symbolism, but its surface meaning is what most concerns me here. Here is Jesus talking alone to a woman, which was shocking enough to his disciples (verse 27) — and a *Samaritan* woman at that. Moreover he asks her for a drink, despite the convention that Jews would not share drinking vessels with Samaritans (verse 10). He engages her in one of his most prolonged reported conversations in the gospels, and he quickly gets around to their religious differences:

> Believe me, the time is coming when you will worship the Father neither on this mountain nor in Jerusalem. You Samaritans worship you know not what: we worship what we know. It is from the Jews that salvation comes. But the time is coming, indeed it is already here, when true worshippers will worship the Father in spirit and in truth. (*John* 4:21-23)

The implication seems to be that although salvation comes from the Jews, it is now available to all. According to *John*, many Samaritans came to believe that Jesus is the Saviour of the world (verses 39-42). As ever, we cannot tell how much in these stories is fact, but these passages suggest a gradual widening of Jesus's concern from Jews to all peoples in the world, as is said explicitly at the end of *Matthew*.

It is surely significant that many of Jesus's most meaningful encounters were with women. In the story of the sisters Mary and Martha, who appear to have been his personal friends (*John* 11:5), he says that Martha is fretting too much about the household tasks, and he commends Mary for leaving them to sit at his feet and listen to his teaching (*Luke* 10:38–42). The moral of the story—not pleasing to the Jews of the time, nor to many Jews and Gentiles since—is surely that whatever the division of labour may be, women should enjoy full equality in all that matters most.

Much of what I have been expounding may seem impressive to contemporary readers, even those of a non-religious or even militantly atheist disposition. But to be honest to the texts, we had better not ignore those bits of Jesus's teaching that seem less attractive to many of us now. He says he has come not to bring peace but a sword, and he warns that families will be divided on his account (*Matthew* 10:34–39; *Luke* 12:49–53). Moreover in each synoptic gospel before the arrest and crucifixion, he comes out with a lengthy apocalyptic discourse, predicting all manner of disasters (*Mark* 13; *Matthew* 24–25; *Luke* 21). Some of this may very probably have been written with the advantage of hindsight, by gospel-writers or compilers ("evangelists" in the old sense of the word) who knew that Jesus had been condemned to death and that the Jewish rebellion in 70 CE had been crushed by the Romans with the total destruction of the Temple.

Some of this apocalyptic material goes beyond even the most disastrous events within human history, and predicts a "Second Coming" of Jesus in supernatural form that will bring an end to human history:

> But in those days, after that distress, the sun will be darkened, the moon will not give her light; the stars will come falling from the sky, the celestial powers will be shaken. Then they will see the Son of Man coming in the clouds with great power and glory, and he will send out the angels and gather his chosen from the four winds, from the farthest bound of earth to the farthest bounds of heaven. (*Mark* 13:24–27; *Matthew* 24:29–31)

One wonders if the evangelists were building too much on a single verse of *Daniel*, itself a recent addition to Hebrew scripture. Matthew had a strong belief in divine judgment, punishment and reward in a life beyond death:

> When the Son of Man comes in his glory and all the angels with him, he will sit on his glorious throne, with all the nations gathered before him. He will separate people into two groups, as a shepherd separates the sheep from the goats; he will place the sheep on his right hand and the goats on his left. Then the king will say to those on his right, "You have

my Father's blessing; come, take possession of the kingdom that has been ready for you since the world was made." ... Then he will say to those on his left, "A curse is on you; go from my sight to the eternal fire that is ready for the devil and his angels". ... And they will go away to eternal punishment but the righteous will enter eternal life. (*Matthew* 25:31–34, 41, 46)

Jesus talks of hell or hell-fire (and the occasional devouring worm) in *Matthew* 5:22, 29–30, 10:28, 18:9, 23:15, 33; *Mark* 9:42–28; and *Luke* 12:5, and there are also references to heaven, or the kingdom of heaven, as a place of reward (*Matthew* 5:12, 8:11). He appears to have believed in an afterlife in which persons carry moral responsibility for their actions in this life, but he does not tell us much about it. When asked a tricky question about the identity and relationships of people in the afterlife, he replies that in the resurrection men and women do not marry, but are like the angels in heaven (*Matthew* 22:30). (See Chapter 10 for my own take on the idea of life after death.)

These eschatological themes are unambiguously there in the gospels, but I dare to suggest that the main thrust of Jesus's ethical teaching does not depend on them. Of course, many Christians accept both, and indeed there have always been some who seem to take the eschatology *more* enthusiastically than the ethics. Apocalyptic end-of-the-world stories have an attraction for a certain kind of mind, and there is usually no arguing people out of it. One can however ask: whatever we may believe or not believe about an end of the world, how should we live with each other in the meantime?

Some comments on Jesus's teaching

Jesus's ethics, if shorn of the eschatology so characteristic of his Jewish context, has much in common with that of Socrates. But it goes beyond the Greeks on the themes of universal love and forgiveness, and in seeing all human life in terms of relation to a personal God whom we can address as Father. Jesus's cognitive style (if I may thus describe it) differs from that of Socrates and Plato. He engages in face-to-face dialogue, to be sure, but he does not go in for the Socratic method of protracted question and answer, and rational even nitpicking debate. He occasionally follows the Jewish practice of debate about how to interpret the sacred texts, but he usually transcends it pretty quickly, and sometimes even contradicts a text.

Two things stand out for me in Jesus's style—his use of parables to suggest a spiritual meaning indirectly, and his extraordinary ability to come out with vivid, memorable turns of phrase that nearly always strike to the spiritual heart of the matter. Again and again, as we have seen, he manages to express his message in a brief and stylish (even pungent) way. This is so characteristic in the gospels, and the phrases used are so original, that we can be pretty confident they come from the historical Jesus. We may describe him as a master of one-liners and sound-bites! But this is not to say that they are all equally successful. "Pay Caesar what belongs to Caesar, and to God what belongs to God" (*Mark* 12:17) seems more like a clever evasion of a difficult question than clear guidance about how to approach money matters. Yet it can provoke thought in those who have ears to hear, and the original hearers would be aware that the emperor's coins labeled him *divi filius*, 'son of a god', suggesting a conflict of religious values and kingdoms. This famous one-liner from Jesus does not tell us what *counts* as God's and what as the government's, but it comes from someone whose message is surely that every aspect of our lives should be brought under the perspective of the Spirit (as Quakers have emphasized).

That illustrates something I want to say in closing this chapter. Many sayings by various people may strike us as deeply insightful, going to the heart of the matter, authoritative in a self-justificatory way. If someone comes out with a *series* of such sayings, we may begin to attribute even more authority to him or her. Indeed many people seem to yearn for a "guru" figure or an authoritative religious tradition to tell them what to believe and what to do. But often people do not agree on *which* sayings or *which* people should carry authority; and it is possible to have second thoughts about someone who has impressed us until now. It is always open to us to use our own intelligence, our experience of life, our common sense, and our pre-existing sense of what is right and wrong, to test what someone says (while admitting that our own judgment is fallible too). If a teacher or guru is willing to engage in open-ended dialogue to answer objections and explain difficulties, their authority can be tested; and if they refuse to engage in any such debate, their authority is diminished. (It is a nice fancy to imagine Jesus and Socrates debating with each other.)

Greek thought puts great store on the intellect, on our ability to attain knowledge of truth, including moral truth (as we will see in the next chapter), and the implication tends to be that the highest fulfillment of human life was attainable only by those who are able to gain such rational knowledge. Jewish thought, and Jesus in particular, puts the emphasis on human goodness, a matter of basic attitude—of "heart" or will rather than mind or intellect—something that is open to all regardless of intellectual ability. We may hope to have both, but if we have to choose between them, Jesus persuades me that we should prefer the latter.

Further reading

There are many different English translations of the Bible (and various denominational preferences between them). One excellent version, which I have quoted from, is the *Oxford Study Bible: Revised English Bible with the Apocrypha*, edited by M.J. Suggs *et al.* (Oxford University Press 1992). This contains explanatory footnotes, and useful essays on the historical, sociological, literary and religious background of the Biblical texts.

The *Gospel of Thomas* has been translated with the rather aggressive title *Jesus untouched by the Church: His Teachings in the Gospel of Thomas*, by Hugh McGregor Ross (York: William Sessions Limited 1998). This edition presents the logia (sayings of Jesus) arranged by theme, in beautiful calligraphy, with helpful explanatory notes.

In Chapters 1–2 of *Beyond Belief: The Secret Gospel of Thomas* (London: Macmillan 2004) Elaine Pagels argues that John's gospel so strongly emphasizing the doctrine of Jesus as incarnate God was written in conscious opposition to the teaching of purely spiritual transformation represented by the gospel of Thomas.

Respectful non-Christian accounts of Jesus's life and teaching are offered by Humphrey Carpenter, *Jesus* (Oxford University Press 1980); and A.N. Wilson, *Jesus* (New York: HarperCollins 1992).

The Meaning of Jesus: Two Visions, by Marcus J. Borg and N.T. Wright (New York: HarperCollins 1999) is an interesting debate between two leading liberal and conservative Christian scholars.

Geza Vermes, in *Jesus the Jew* (New York: Macmillan 1973) and *Jesus and the World of Judaism* (London: SCM Press 1983), brings to bear his expertise in ancient Judaism to argue that the historical Jesus was a Galilean teacher and healer, a Jewish figure quite different from the incarnational interpretation that has been put on him by Christianity ever since Paul.

CHAPTER 4
ANCIENT PHILOSOPHIES OF LIFE

The world of multicultural empires

Let us go back to ancient Greece (a culture of which Jesus seems to have known nothing) in which there had already been a golden age of philosophy, inaugurated by Socrates. In the next two generations there arose the towering intellectual figures of Plato (427–347 BCE) and Aristotle (384–322 BCE); and Greek philosophical thought continued to develop for many centuries thereafter, well into the Christian era. After Aristotle's time the lively but quarrelsome little city-states of Greece gave way to world-conquering empires. In the 4th century BCE Alexander the Great led his Macedonian armies all over the Middle East and as far as India, implanting Hellenic (Greek-derived) culture over the region. The new city named after him, Alexandria in Egypt, became a centre of Hellenism. Then in the 2nd century BCE the Romans conquered Greece, and went on to acquire the greatest empire the West had known.

In this new "cosmopolitan" world the cultures and religions of smaller communities were mingled and mangled, and the emphasis of philosophical discussion shifted away from the high metaphysical theories of Plato and Aristotle towards a concentration on practical instruction on how best to live. There developed a variety of philosophical "schools" (and they were teaching institutions, not just schools of thought) offering their versions of practical wisdom, or philosophy of life—the most famous being Plato's Academy, Aristotle's Lyceum, and the Stoic and Epicurean schools that followed. These were still based in Athens, but schools also grew up elsewhere, especially in Rome, where the more cultured of the Romans derived much of their education from Greece.

Christianity emerged into this multicultural world of the Roman Empire, and had to compete both with many other religious cults and with the schools of philosophy. The early "church fathers" debated what attitude to take to this immensely influential Greek philosophical tradition that pre-dated Christianity, and then as now, theologians differed sharply over how Christianity should relate to other schools of thought. Origen tried to use Greek philosophical concepts to express Christian beliefs, but Tertullian expressed the most uncompromising attitude when he famously asked: "What has Athens got to do with Jerusalem?"—a rhetorical question to which he obviously expected the answer "Nothing"! The whole trend of this book is to argue that he was wrong, that religious belief should not be insulated from philosophical thought, and that we all need to be open to new light from whatever source it may come.

Plato

Like Socrates, Plato was convinced that it is possible by the assiduous use of our reason to attain knowledge of deep-lying truths about the world and human nature, and to apply this knowledge for the benefit of society. One of the most famous of his dialogues is the *Republic*. In this wide-ranging work he touches on metaphysics, theory of knowledge, psychology, morals, politics, social structure, the family, education, the arts, and the afterlife—but the main theme is his prescription for an ideal human society (hence the title). One crucial thread of his argument is an answer to the challenge posed at the outset, that "justice" is merely a covering word for the advantage of the stronger. Plato proposes to show that despite appearances, it is in the long-term interest of everyone to be "just" or moral, and he does this by rethinking what justice or morality or well-being is: in the individual, it consists in a harmony of the three different elements in our souls, namely reason, emotion and desire. But this can only be attained if there is a similar harmony in society, with the three classes of rulers, soldiers and labourers working together for the common good. In the central metaphysical sections of the *Republic* Plato insists on a very theoretical conception of reason as consisting in knowledge of the "Forms", i.e. the abstract universals lying behind everything we think about. Such specialized knowledge needs a highly-educated elite (the "philosopher-kings") who, he controversially claims, are the only people fit to rule society.

We may suspect that Plato over-intellectualizes the role of reason. Is a higher education either necessary or sufficient for effective political office? Indeed, is high intelligence necessary or sufficient for goodness? Yet elsewhere he shows awareness that the pursuit of virtue requires more than reasoning: although he was himself a great writer, indeed a stupendous generator of difficult texts, he tended to agree with Socrates that actual dialogue is the best way to get people to think for themselves and perhaps change their approach to life. In his famous and stylish drinking-dialogue, the *Symposium*, Plato enlarges on the theme of Love, in various senses of the word. When it is Socrates' turn to give a speech he reports a lesson from a wise woman to the effect that our erotic love for beautiful bodies needs to be transformed into a higher kind of love for the Form of Beauty itself:

> This is what it is to go aright, or be led by another, into the mystery of Love: one goes always upward for the sake of this Beauty, starting out from beautiful things and using them like rising stairs: from one body to two and from two to all beautiful bodies, then from beautiful bodies to beautiful customs, and from customs to learning beautiful things, and from these lessons he arrives in the end at this lesson, which is learning of this very Beauty, so that in the end he comes to know just what it is to be beautiful.

> ... how would it be ... if someone got to see the Beautiful itself, absolute, pure, unmixed, not polluted by human flesh or colour or any other great nonsense of mortality, but if he could see the divine Beauty itself in its one form? ... in that life alone, when he looks at Beauty in the only way that Beauty can be seen—only then will it become possible for him to give birth not to images of virtue ... but to true virtue. (*Symposium* 211-212)

In the Republic it is the Form of the Good that is pre-eminent: it plays an almost God-like role in Plato's philosophy, being described as the source of all reality, truth, and goodness. He compares the role of the Good in the world of the Forms to that of the sun as the source of all light in the world of material things. The twin images of sun and cave—the source of light, and the darkness of our unenlightened state—give us a memorable picture of the human condition:

> So that what gives truth to the things known and the power to know to the knower is the form of the Good. And though it is the cause of knowledge and truth, it is also an object of knowledge. Both Knowledge and Truth are beautiful things, but the good is other and more beautiful

> than they. In the visible realm, light and sight are rightly considered sunlike, but it is wrong to think that they are the sun, so here it is right to think of Knowledge and Truth as good like but wrong to think that either of them is the Good—for the Good is yet more prized. (*Republic* 508d-e)

Plato thus offers us a vision of intellectual and spiritual progress towards the transcendent, a hope of "seeing the Light" (with a capital L).

It is easy to see how those Jews and Christians who had some education in Greek philosophy might want to identify Plato's form of the Good with God. But the Jewish and Greek traditions have very different notions of the divine, for the Hebrew Scriptures are full of stories of God speaking to individuals and acting in the world, conceptions which are quite foreign to Greek philosophy: Plato certainly did not conceive of the form of the Good intervening in the world. Philo, a Greek-educated Jew who lived in Alexandria around the time of Jesus, tried to synthesize the two traditions. He made much of the personified female figure of Wisdom in some of the late Jewish scriptures, and even called the Word or *logos* "the first-begotten of God", son of God by the virgin Wisdom. Philo did not impress his fellow-Jews, but the influence of such ideas on early Christianity is obvious, especially in the mention of the eternal Word in the prologue to John's gospel.

Some six or seven centuries after Plato, towards the end of the ancient era, there was a remarkable flowering of neo-Platonic thought. The most famous name here is Plotinus (3rd century CE) who developed Plato's notion of the pre-eminence of the form of the Good into an elaborate doctrine of a transcendent God as the source of all being and knowledge. The implication for us is that we are capable of an ascent towards the divine that can culminate in a state of mystical union with God. Plotinus's thought had much in common with Christianity, though strangely he does not show any awareness of the new religion. This neo-Platonism was a major influence on St. Augustine, and hence on the middle ages and even down to our own day.

Aristotle

Aristotle was educated in Plato's Academy, and though deeply influenced by Plato he criticized him on some important points. For a few years he was tutor to the teenager who grew up to become Alexander the Great—although displaying little influence from his distinguished philosophical teacher! Aristotle did extensive research on the structure of animals and plants, and this experience of empirical scientific work shows in his writings, which display a more scientific and this-worldly spirit compared with Plato's yearning for transcendence. The Aristotelian texts that have come down to us cover an amazing range of subjects—logic, metaphysics, epistemology, astronomy, physics, meteorology, biology, psychology, ethics, aesthetics, politics—and in many of these he was a pioneer.

The *Nicomachean Ethics* is the main work in which Aristotle discusses human life, its ideals and its problems. He gives an account of the purpose of life, and how it can be put into practice. Where most religions offer an otherworldly kind of salvation, Aristotle offers a much more "humanist" or "secular" account of human fulfillment, appropriate to our unique capacity for reason. The message that emerges is: (a) human fulfillment consists in the active exercise of our faculties, not in mere passive enjoyment; (b) it must involve the use of our rational capacity; (c) this activity should be conducted "well and finely", displaying the best, most complete kind of "excellence" or virtue; and (d) it should last over a lifetime.

Plato had defended the dualist view according to which the human soul can exist apart from the body after death. But Aristotle radically undermines this whole way of thinking in his short treatise *de Anima* ("Of the soul"). Here his biological thinking makes a vital contribution to philosophy. He sees human beings as one kind of animal—a very special kind, capable of rational thought. The human soul or mind should be understood not as a detachable thing, but as a cluster of rational faculties (including language-use) that are distinctive of the human way of living. On this conception, it makes no sense to talk of soul or mind existing apart from the body, for if there is no living body there is no mental functioning at all.

In the last book of the *Ethics* a comparison with "the gods" enters into Aristotle's argument (though one wonders how literally he takes them):

> If, then intelligence is something divine as compared to a human being, so too a life in accordance with this will be divine as compared to a human life. One should not follow the advice of those who say "Human you are, think human thoughts", and "Mortals you are, think mortal ones", but instead, so far as is possible, assimilate to the immortals and

do everything with the aim of living in accordance with what is highest of the things in us; for even if it is small in bulk, the degree to which it surpasses everything in power and dignity is far greater. (*Nicomachean Ethics* 1177b31ff)

Here Aristotle displays the influence of Plato's quasi-religious ideal that we should cultivate the highest aspects of our human nature, and aspire towards standards or ideals that are in some sense superhuman. But Aristotle's gods (if he takes them seriously at all) seem to be purely intellectual beings, who do not care at all about human affairs, whereas the Hebrew God was a God of love as well as knowledge and power, who cares about social justice, and is capable of forgiveness—and this carries over to the Christian conception.

Epicureanism

As the city-states of ancient Greece were absorbed into a cosmopolitan society, philosophy took a more practical, quasi-religious direction, and the abstract theorizing of Plato and Aristotle tended to be passed over. People looked to philosophy (the Greek word means "the love of wisdom") not so much for theoretical pronouncements but for guidance as to how life should best be lived in an unstable and bewildering new world. Epicurus lived in the 4th–3rd centuries BCE. He was inclined to the sceptical view that we cannot know anything about the world beyond what is given to sense-perception, but he held that the most likely view is that nothing exists except matter and space, and that all material bodies are composed of eternal, indestructible atoms. Even the mind or soul is composed of atoms, in a sort of gaseous form, and it cannot survive the death of the body. To this very modern-sounding materialism, Epicurus added a modern-sounding twist: to leave room for human freewill and moral responsibility, he postulated that atoms perform unpredictable "swerves" as they fall through space—which can be seen as a primitive anticipation of the probabilistic uncertainties of quantum mechanics!

Epicurus's main message was that the point of philosophy is to free men from fear, above all from fear of the gods. Perhaps prudently, he did not deny that gods exist, but merely said that the world is not created or ruled by them, they are too sensible to bother themselves with the affairs of men, and the world is too muddled and disordered to be a divine creation. Epicurus's main concern was with the means of attaining happiness. His "philosophy" is usually said to be that pleasure is the ultimate goal of life—but that is a misleading oversimplification, for he was far from recommending the unthinking hedonistic pursuit of pleasures of the moment. Sensual pleasures are not bad in themselves, and there is a place for them in a good life, but what Epicurus prescribed was a careful, prudent search for permanent "serenity of soul", with the minimum of pain and a reasonable measure of the kind of moderate pleasures that do not undermine one's continuing well-being. Wisdom is needed to free us from bondage to the passions, from fear of the gods, and from the fear of death, which is only extinction, not survival into another world.

The practical results may not be very different from those of Stoicism, as we shall see. But there is a difference of emphasis. Epicureanism sounds ultimately selfish, in that virtue comes into the story only as a means to one's own happiness, whereas in Stoicism happiness is allowed only as a by-product of virtue. Epicureanism is perhaps the most prevalent "philosophy of life" of our own time (though not under that name, for not many people have heard of it!). Its attractions are obvious, but on reflection it is in danger of being self-centred, for there seems to be little concern for other people or for social justice except in so far as the fate of others may impinge on one's own lifestyle. Moreover it seems to offer no purpose in life beyond self-preservation and enjoyment: but if such wants are supplied and there is a lack of aspiration towards anything higher, boredom threatens; and out of boredom, evil can come.

Stoicism

The founder of Stoicism was Zeno, who set up his own school in Athens in the 3rd century BCE. Apparently he discouraged young men from attending, because he thought that only mature men could understand philosophy (we can be pretty certain from what we know of Greek culture that there was no question of women listening in, however mature they may have been!). He taught for some thirty or forty years, and acquired a reputation for the consistency of his temperate life with his philosophy.

Although Zeno and the later Stoics developed theories about logic and natural science, they are most famous for their ethics, summed up in the prescription that life should be lived consistently "according to nature". But everything depends on what is meant by "nature" here. The basic Stoic idea was that there is a rational principle or "Seminal Reason" that rules the universe, and of which the rational human soul is a sort of seed. They talked rather indifferently of God or Nature, which suggests a pantheist philosophy in which the two are identified. They did not ridicule traditional religious faiths, but suggested allegorical interpretations of them to make them consistent with philosophy. Stoic morality can thus be described either as willing surrender to divine will and providence, or as rational recognition of how things are in the world and disciplining ourselves, especially our emotions, to recognize reality and live in accordance with it. The *Hymn* of Cleanthes (Zeno's successor as head of the Stoic school) would not be out of place amongst the *Psalms*, if we replace Zeus by Lord:

> Thou, O Zeus, are praised above all gods:
> many are thy names and thine is all power for ever.
>
> The beginning of the world was from thee:
> and with law thou rulest over all things. ...
>
> Nor is anything done upon the earth apart from thee;
> nor in the firmament, nor in the seas:
> Save that which the wicked do: but their own folly.
>
> But thine is the skill to set even the crooked straight ...
>
> Let folly be dispersed from our souls;
> that we may repay thee the honour wherewith thou has honoured us:
> Singing praise of thy works for ever; as becometh the sons of men.

Philo had tried to connect Judaism with Platonic philosophy, but Cleanthes' hymn seems to me to make a closer connection between Judaism and Stoicism, which suggests that the spiritual attitudes of worshipfulness and acknowledgment of human failings can be shared despite differences of theology.

Stoicism holds that happiness is *not* to be found in pleasure (not even in the careful, moderate pursuit of pleasure that Epicurus recommended), but rather in the rational adjustment of our aims, feelings and conduct to the laws and purposes of the universe. There is much in the world that we cannot change and must learn to live with; our only choice is how *well* we make the necessary adjustments. So we must use our rational powers to control our own attitudes and emotions, and ideally to *eradicate* our emotions (though that hardly seems possible, and perhaps not even desirable!). But that is the limit of our freedom; everything else is governed by the laws of God or Nature. If suffering affects good men, it is be only temporary, and cannot be evil. Like Jews and Christians, the Stoic is committed to believing that everything ultimately happens for the best, even if we cannot see how what appears to us as pain, suffering and evil fits into the big picture, which is in some sense divinely-ordained. Another prayer of Cleanthes approximates to monotheist spirituality in its submission to "divine will":

> Lead me, Zeus, and you too, Destiny,
> To wherever your decrees have assigned me.
> I follow readily, but if I choose not,
> Wretched though I am, I must follow still.
> Fate guides the willing, but drags the unwilling.

Stoicism holds that we are free only to change ourselves. But it follows from that that we are always capable of virtue, no matter what befalls us: even in prison or in the torture-chamber we have a choice what attitude to take, and we remain capable of heroism. We may not be lucky enough to enjoy happiness, but we can always attain that inner satisfaction which comes from knowing that we have done the right thing, hence that paradigm Stoic saying: "virtue is its own reward". In an uncertain and unstable ancient world, Stoicism appealed to those (presumably the majority) who were not in the fortunate position of being able to practise the prudent pursuit of pleasure recommended by Epicureanism. It also partially anticipated Christianity in spiritual attitude.

Roman Stoicism

Rome grew steadily in military power until by the second century CE it had imposed its rule over most of Europe, North Africa and the Middle East. The highly-disciplined and well-equipped Roman armies were practically invincible, but in terms of high culture (philosophy, science, and the arts) Rome was largely outclassed by the Greek society they had conquered. Well-off Romans would send their sons to be educated in the philosophical schools of Athens.

Traditional Roman religion believed in spirits of the seasons, of nature, of procreation, or of virtues. In the Roman home, the undying fire in the hearth represented the goddess Vesta who symbolized the life and continuity of the family. There were festivals, rites and sacrifices to a variety of spirits, including those representing Rome itself. There was a hierarchy of priests and "colleges", topped out with a *pontifex maximus* (which seems to have influenced the hierarchical structure of Roman Catholicism much later). The traditional upbringing, morality and religion contributed to the archetypical Roman character—orderly and severe, loyal and reverent, tenacious and brave—that enabled Rome to conquer the world.

But this was true only of old republican Rome, before the era of Caesars and Emperors. As the conquests proceeded, they brought more and more of the world into the Roman economic system. Food and slaves were imported, and the taxes levied on the conquered territories enabled an extraordinary degree of luxury amongst the upper classes. Well-off Romans (rather like the modern West) got used to the idea that the rest of the world owed them a living—there were spacious villas and hot baths, sumptuous banquets and domestic artwork, grandiose architecture and arenas for violent gladiatorial contests, like the Colosseum whose enormous ruins still exist in Rome. But the displaced people from many countries formed an unstable underclass, whose support was sought by ambitious politicians who entertained them with gladiator shows of unspeakable cruelty to men and beasts. Overeating and sexual license became fashionable amongst the rich, and infanticide and abortion were so widely practised that the stability of the traditional family was undermined. Political conflicts were increasingly solved by civil war or assassination (Julius Caesar providing the most famous example of both). There was almost a competition in inventing new forms of gruesome torture for prisoners or political opponents. Admittedly, Roman rule brought peace and prosperity to many of the provinces, for some of the time. There were some wise emperors who provided stable administration, such as Augustus, Trajan, Hadrian and the stoical Marcus Aurelius, but there were many more who drenched the world in blood. It seems fair to say that at the heart of this greatest of Western empires there was corruption, which led to its decline and eventual fall.

It was not all corruption, however. There were some notable Roman statesmen, philosophers and poets, artists and architects. Lucretius (1st century BCE) managed to be both a philosopher and a poet of distinction, a distinction practically unrivalled in history. *The Nature of Things* is a book-length poem expounding his version of the Epicurean philosophy. He sings of the irrelevance of the traditional gods, of the atomistic natural philosophy and the material nature of the soul (none of which are obvious topics for poetry!), and he argues passionately that since death is extinction, there is nothing to be feared from it.

Although Epicureanism may have been found sympathetic by the hedonists of Rome, Stoicism became more attractive when times got harder for many. It found eloquent expression in the letters of Seneca (1st century CE) who became an advisor to the notorious Emperor Nero. He wrote of God in what can seem like Christian terms, although he seems unaware of Christianity:

> God is near you, is with you, is inside you. ... No man is good, indeed, without God — is anyone capable of rising above fortune unless he has help from God? (*Letter* XLI)

> One can do nothing better than endure what cannot be cured and attend uncomplainingly the God at whose instance all things come about (*Letter* CVII)

In places he approaches very close to the ethical teaching of Jesus:

> No one can live a happy life if he thinks only of himself and turns everything to his own purposes. You should live for the other person if you wish to live for yourself. (*Letter* XLVIII)

> A good character is the only guarantee of everlasting, carefree happiness. (*Letter* XXVII)

Seneca was a rich Roman who got involved in high politics, and when he fell out of favour with the inconstant Nero, the emperor commanded him to commit suicide, which he duly did.

Stoicism was also expounded by Epictetus (2nd century CE), a freed slave who insisted that *all* humans are "children of Zeus" and have the capacity for virtue. Here was a universal ethic that could appeal to all classes and peoples, as Christianity did. The Stoic philosophy of life was most famously expressed in the *Meditations* of Marcus Aurelius (2nd century CE), the only Roman Emperor who can count as a philosopher:

> Nothing is more melancholy than to compass the whole creation ... without once understanding that to hold fast to the divine spirit within, and serve it loyally, is all that is needful. Such service involves keeping it pure from passion, and from aimlessness, and from discontent with the works of gods or men ... (*Meditations* II.13)

> Strive your hardest to be such a man as Philosophy would have you to be. Reverence the gods, succour your fellow-mortals. Life is short, and this earthly existence has but a single fruit to yield — holiness within, and selfless action without. (*Meditations* VI.30)

But Aurelius's compassion sounds dutiful rather than loving, and there is a world-weary streak in his writing:

> What is evil? A thing you have seen times out of number. Likewise with every other sort of occurrence also, be prompt to remind yourself that this, too, you have witnessed many times before. For everywhere, above and below, you will find nothing but the selfsame things; they fill the pages of all history, ancient, modern, and contemporary, and they fill our cities and homes today. There is no such thing as novelty; all is as trite as it is transitory. (*Meditations* VII.1)

More than once Aurelius echoes *Ecclesiastes* in the Hebrew Scriptures:

> All things are wearisome. No one can describe them all, no eye can see them all, no ear can hear them all. What has happened will happen again, and what has been done will be done again; there is nothing new under the sun. (*Ecclesiastes* 1:8–9)

This is a mood to which we are all subject at times. But in the Bible it is counteracted both in the Old Testament: "I shall pour out my spirit on your offspring, and my blessing on your children"(*Isaiah* 44:3), and in the New, with the insistence that God has acted decisively to redeem the world in Christ: there is a theme of hope and joy that is conspicuous by its absence from Stoicism.

It is remarkable how many anticipations of Christianity can be found in these ancient philosophies—a sign, to my mind, that spiritual wisdom is not unique to any one school of thought, that deficiencies in one may be corrected or enriched by another, and that we cannot afford to reject or completely neglect any of them. But this was not the attitude of Justinian, the Christian emperor in Constantinople in the early 6th century CE, who closed the ancient schools because they were pagan institutions. The long story of the ancient Greek and Roman world was finally over, and Europe was entering the thoroughly Christianized medieval era, centred on the Roman papacy in the West and the Byzantine Empire in the East.

Further reading

Will Durant, *The Story of Civilization, Part II: The Life of Greece*, and *Part III: Caesar and Christ* (New York: Simon & Schuster, 1939 and 1944). This sweeping, magisterial and graceful study (whose continuation goes up to the 19th century) gives prominence to the life of the mind. I have re-used a few apposite phrases from it.

Pierre Hadot, *Philosophy as a Way of Life: Spiritual Exercises from Socrates to Foucault* (Blackwell 1995)

I provide compact introductions to the philosophies of Plato and Aristotle in *Twelve Theories of Human Nature*, by Leslie Stevenson and David Haberman, 6th edition (New York: Oxford University Press 2012).

In Oxford University Press's Very Short Introduction series, there are books on *Ancient Philosophy* and on *Plato* by Julia Annas, on *Aristotle* by Jonathan Barnes.

Seneca, *Letters from a Stoic*, translated by Robin Campbell (Harmondsworth: Penguin 1969)

Marcus Aurelius, *Meditations*, translated by Maxwell Staniforth (Harmondsworth: Penguin 1964)

Robert Graves' historical novels *I, Claudius* and *Claudius the God* give a vivid picture of the glories and depravities of life at the top in Rome, around the time of Jesus.

CHAPTER 5

RATIONALISM OR FUNDAMENTALISM
RECURRING TENSIONS IN CHRISTIANITY, ISLAM AND JUDAISM

In Chapter 3 I tried to write about Jesus without presupposing the doctrines of Christianity, the religion that sprang up in his name soon after his death. But that was a difficult aim, for the original Jesus has been buried under two millennia of controversial theological and ecclesiastical developments. In this chapter I am going to present a bird's eye view (no doubt by a biased bird, who may know only a little more than most readers, and less than some!) of an enormous stretch of human religious history—no less than the development of Christianity, Islam and Judaism (three religions with a common Semitic root) from the 1st century up to about 1500. I hope this will provide a more informed and sympathetic view than the more exclusive views of themselves usually offered by these three traditions.

Christianity—the first three centuries

Jesus was seen as a dangerous trouble-maker by the Jewish and Roman authorities, and was crucified at their behest in Jerusalem around 30 CE. Immediately afterwards, according to the *Acts of the Apostles*, his disciples began proclaiming that by the crucifixion and alleged resurrection of Jesus, God had fulfilled ancient Jewish prophecies of the coming of the Messiah and the pouring out of God's Holy Spirit. Peter said the resurrected Jesus was now "exalted at God's right hand" (*Acts* 2:33)—high status indeed, but not yet a claim that Jesus was to be identified as God Himself. This new cult of the risen Jesus rapidly gained converts, initially within Judaism, but later all round the Mediterranean.

I will postpone discussion of the idea of resurrection until Chapter 10; but we should note that the theme of a god dying and coming to life again and offering eternal life to his devotees was already present in several pre-Christian religions. There was the Greek cult of Dionysus which the Roman Senate, getting nervous about the multiculturalism of its day, tried to suppress in the 2nd century BCE. In Syria the god Tammuz was hailed with the cry "Adonis is risen". In the cult of Cybele, worshippers mourned the death of her beloved Attis, only to celebrate his resurrection on the morrow, with the renewal of the earth. There was a parallel theme in the Egyptian religion of Isis and her son Osiris that spread to many parts of the Roman Empire (Isis was even hailed as "Mother of God", anticipating the status later ascribed to Mary). I am not suggesting that these anthropological data disprove Christian claims, for Christian theologians can always argue that *they* have the real truth and the pagan versions are mere anticipations or echoes of it. No doubt there is a natural origin for the idea of resurrection in the annual "death and rebirth" of the sun in mid-winter (Christianized as Christmas), and the renewed growth in spring (hence Easter), but that does not show that there is no valid spiritual interpretation of resurrection. A distinguished historian has summed up the story of early Christianity like this:

> Christianity arose out of Jewish apocalyptic—esoteric revelations of the coming Kingdom; it derived its impetus from the personality and vision of Christ; it gained strength from the belief in his resurrection, and the promise of eternal life; it received doctrinal form in the theology of Paul; it grew by the absorption of pagan faith and ritual; it became a triumphant Church by inheriting the organizing patterns and genius of Rome. (Will Durant, *The Story of Civilization, Part III; Caesar and Christ*, p. 575)

The first proclaimers of Christ were Jews; they went to the Temple in Jerusalem every day, they adhered to the Jewish laws, and preached their faith only to Jews. They claimed to have received miraculous powers of healing and speech from Christ or his Holy Spirit (Acts 1–5). But as the new sect grew, the Jewish authorities got alarmed and brought some of the leaders to trial; Stephen defied them, and became the first Christian martyr (Acts 6–7). Some Christians fled Jerusalem and established new communities in Samaria and Antioch; Peter got as far as Rome, where he made converts and was martyred. James the brother of Jesus became head of the Jewish Christians, but in 62 he too was put to death. A few years later the Jewish uprising against Roman rule resulted in utter defeat and the destruction of the Second Temple. The surviving Jews scattered as refugees, and Judaism and Christianity parted in mutual recrimination, which has continued down the centuries with tragic consequences.

St. Paul was the greatest theorist of early Christianity: it is only a little of an exaggeration to say that he created Christian theology single-handed. The relation between Paul and Jesus bears some analogy to that between Plato and Socrates. In each case, the older man did not leave any writings, so for knowledge of him and his teaching we have to depend largely on his successors (including the gospel-writers in the case of Jesus, and Xenophon in the case of Socrates). And in each case the younger man's theories seem to go beyond anything his master actually said (which does not mean that they are false, just that they are original). Paul was a Jew of great ability and energy who began his career by persecuting the Christians (*Acts* Ch. 9). But after his famous conversion on the road to Damascus, when he claimed to have been personally confronted by the risen Christ, he became the foremost Christian missionary, journeying all round the Eastern Mediterranean and ending up in Rome.

Paul's letters or "epistles" to the early Christian communities have been, along with the gospels, some of the most influential writings of all history. Surprisingly, he shows little knowledge of Jesus's *teaching*, which we reviewed in Chapter 3: he concentrates on the claimed salvation of the world by Jesus's crucifixion and resurrection, laying the foundations of subsequent Christian theology by emphasizing the divine person and cosmic role of Jesus. He conveys a charismatic sense that God has done something of world-changing importance through the death and resurrection of Jesus, who Paul now identifies as God's Son (whatever that means—see below). In *Romans* Paul expounds at length his understanding that the sacrificial death of Jesus has brought about salvation from the universal human condition of sin (the atonement). His thinking is strongly influenced by the Jewish tradition in which he had been educated, but he rejects Judaism's claim to special access to God, and says that the salvation God offers in Christ is now available to all humanity. He is hard on backsliders, sectarians, heretics, sexual relations outside marriage, and on homosexuals. Despite what he says about men and women being equal in Christ (*Galatians* 3:28) he does not seem to accept its full implications (*1 Corinthians* 11:3–16); and he does not question the institution of slavery. But his sense of divine grace and love blows away that world-weary mood that we have found in Stoicism:

> Therefore, now that we have been justified through faith, we are at peace with God through our Lord Jesus Christ, who has given us access to that grace in which we now live; and we exult in the hope of the divine glory that is to be ours. (*Romans* 5:1–2)

> Put on, then, garments that suit God's chosen and beloved people: compassion, kindness, humility, gentleness, patience … to bind everything together there must be love. … Always be thankful. Let the gospel of Christ dwell among you in all its richness … sing from the heart in gratitude to God. (*Colossians* 3:12–16)

Paul's great hymn to faith, hope and love (*1 Corinthians* 13) is too familiar to need quoting here. Similar thoughts about divine love are to be found in the letters ascribed to John, who said that God *is* love (*1 John* 4:8). It is not difficult to understand why Christianity was attractive to so many people in the ancient world, in contrast to the corruptions and cruelties of Rome. It is harder to explain why Christians should have been so persecuted, except as an instance of the sadly ubiquitous human tendency to bully those who differ from the prevailing norm, especially if they are seen as a threat to the existing power-structure.

But Christianity was not without its internal problems. It is clear that the early Christians expected an imminent end to history, when Christ would return in glory, fulfilling ancient eschatological prediction. Jesus himself is reported as predicting the end of the world in *Matthew* Ch. 24, though much of that chapter would seem to refer to the destruction of the Jewish Temple that occurred after Jesus's death, but which the writer of *Matthew* must have known about. In a letter attributed to Peter we read that "on the day of the Lord … the heavens will disappear with a great rushing sound" (*2 Peter* 3:10). And Paul keeps telling his readers that the time is short, and in one of his earliest letters he gave a dramatic physical description of what he expected:

> When God's trumpet sounds, then the Lord himself will descend from heaven; first the Christian dead will rise, then we who are still alive

shall join them, caught up in the clouds to meet the Lord in the air. Thus we shall always be with the Lord. (*1 Thessalonians* 4:16-17)

But the fact is no such apocalyptic event has occurred, so Christians had to get used to the idea that they were going to have to live out their lives in the world as they knew it. Despite the predictions of various millennarian sects down the centuries, the end of the world has still not arrived—though the latest cult will no doubt claim that it is definitely coming *this* time! It remains orthodox Christian doctrine that God will eventually bring the world of human history to an end (in what theologians like to call "the eschaton"), but the mainstream denominations do not seem to expect it any time soon. The early Christian communities began to organize themselves in structure and in belief. The system of deacons, priests, and bishops emerged, and the practice of the sacraments, especially baptism and the eucharist of bread and wine. But theological controversies soon began to divide Christians, as they have done ever since.

In the first two centuries there developed an opposition between "gnostic" and orthodox interpretations of Christianity. The term "gnostic" comes from a Greek word for knowledge, but in religious usage it came to be associated with claims of direct (mystical) experience of God or divine realities. There was a bewildering variety of gnostic cults or "mystery religions" around the Middle East, each offering its own kind of esoteric religious knowledge for its initiates. Amongst those claiming to be Christian, various texts now known as "gnostic gospels" circulated, and since that jarful of ancient texts turned up in the sands of Egypt in 1945, we now know a good deal more about them. Gnostically-inclined Christians could find support in a purely spiritual interpretation of Jesus's talk of "the kingdom of God", e.g. in *Luke* 17:20-21, as well as in the *Gospel of Thomas* (as we saw in Chapter 3). They could also appeal to the pouring out of the Holy Spirit reported in Acts, and to much of Paul's writing if spiritually rather than metaphysically interpreted, such as the verses quoted above and "In Christ Jesus the life-giving law of the Spirit has set you free from the law of sin and death" (*Romans* 8:2).

However a different interpretation was to win out in the sometimes bitter controversies within Christianity in the first three centuries. It was represented by the gospel of John which strongly emphasizes the full divinity of Jesus; and it was decisively led by Irenaeus, Bishop of Lyons, towards end of the 2nd century. Our word 'irenical', meaning *peaceful*, is related to his name—but if Elaine Pagels and other scholars are right, he achieved peace and unity in the Western church by resolute suppression of different tendencies within Christianity that he called "heretic" and "schismatic". Irenaeus was dealt a difficult hand by history: he witnessed the cruel martyrdom of Christian bishops and their followers, and then found himself at a young age leader of his own community. But Christendom, while being forcibly suppressed by the Romans, was also subject to severe internal divisions, with all sorts of groups claiming to experience renewed outpourings of the Holy Spirit. The obvious problem arose (and it is still very much with us even now): who can tell when the Holy Spirit stops, or which are its genuinely-inspired manifestations? Irenaeus percipiently asked "How can we tell the difference between the word of God and merely human words?" (I will revisit this question in connection with Quaker claims to experience of divine Light in Chapters 6–8.)

Irenaeus's response was to appeal to what he took to be the central elements of the Christian tradition as it had developed so far. He was dismayed by the plethora of sects and cults that claimed to be Christian, and he was especially suspicious of those gnostics who offered a second baptism for those who seemed to have acquired the alleged secret knowledge. (One might sympathize with the thought that there should be no such distinction between "primitive" and "advanced" Christians.) Irenaeus found time to compose a massive five-volume treatise aggressively entitled *Refutation and Overthrow of Falsely So-called Knowledge*. He was tremendously influential towards unifying Western Christians in one "catholic" (universal) church, in confirming the canon of the New Testament and suppressing rival gospels, and in commending one way of interpreting the approved books. But unattractive as some of the rival religious tendencies may have been, there may have been a danger of losing the baby with the bathwater. There often seems to be a tension in religion between dogmatic theology and lived experience, as we will see in the rest of this chapter. In Chapter 6 I will look at the Quaker attempt to tilt the balance towards personal experience.

There was also controversy at the theological level about the relationship between Christianity and Greek philosophy. Justin Martyr (2nd century) was prepared to adopt as Christian "whatever all people have said well", especially Platonic philosophy. But Tertullian (2nd–3rd centuries) was ferocious in defence of what he saw as Christian distinctiveness, and famously asked "What has Athens to do with

Jerusalem?" He turned his back on human reasoning, and rejoiced in what he saw as the authority of divine revelation alone:

> God's son died: it is believable precisely because it is absurd. He was buried and rose again: it is certain because it is impossible.

Tertullian also described women as "the gate by which the demon enters", thus displaying a tendency to denigrate (or fear?) women, which has shown itself repeatedly in some strands of Christianity (and in other world cultures). At the end of his ultra-orthodox career he threw in his lot with some of the schismatics that Irenaeus was battling with.

At the other extreme from Tertullian was Origen (2nd-3rd centuries), an omnivorous reader of both Christian and pagan literature. He prepared a revised Greek version of the Bible, and wrote voluminous commentaries on it, using an allegorical method of interpretation according to which moral and spiritual meanings are to be found underlying the literal meaning, which can then be passed over. Like Augustine two centuries later, Origen suggested that the *Genesis* story of creation and many subsequent miracle stories need not be literally true (thus pulling the rug from under the feet of modern-day "creationists" who think that Christianity requires them to reject the theory of evolution). Yet doubts were raised about Origen's own orthodoxy, and though he died to all intents a martyr's death, his opinions were later condemned by the Church. Then as now, there was tension and oscillation between rationalist and fundamentalist tendencies within the Church, and original thinkers have fallen off the swaying tightrope of Christian orthodoxy on one side or the other.

The Council of Nicea

Let us now see how Christianity came to *power*. Though the late Roman Empire tolerated a variety of religious cults, it demanded total subservience to the Emperor in all political matters. In the effort to shore up their faltering regimes, some emperors tried to revive traditional Roman religion, while others encouraged or enforced a cult of Emperor-worship. Christians stubbornly insisted that they had a higher allegiance to Christ, and despite persecutions and cruel martyrdoms they grew in number, at a time when the power and prestige of the Empire was weakening. By about 300 they had become so numerous and influential that the Emperor Constantine decided that since he couldn't beat them he had better join them, and in 323 he proclaimed himself a Christian and invited his subjects to follow his example. Whatever his motivation, it was a fateful decision, for from that day forward European Christianity was incorporated into the power-structure. It survived the demise of the Roman Empire, with the Roman Papacy living on like its spiritual ghost with prestige and power, at least until the Reformation. Christianity has retained official influence in several European states into modern times.

Christianity radically changed the Empire, but Rome also affected Christianity—or at least the Western Catholic version of Christianity (there were Christian communities as far afield as Armenia, Ethiopia, and South India that were never part of the Roman deal). One of Constantine's first moves was to call a General Council of the Christian churches, which met at Nicea (now Iznik in Turkey) in the year 325. It seems he had no particular interest in theology, but wanted the divergent churches to stabilize his newly Christianized regime by agreeing on a common set of beliefs, so he sent his imperial commissioners to the Council to make sure that the assembled bishops did not go away before they had thrashed out a creed.

In the preceding three centuries the first Christian theologians ("the church fathers") had entered into intricate debates, often trying to formulate Christian beliefs in the terminology of Greek philosophy. The central issue at Nicea was the precise nature of Jesus Christ. Jesus had addressed God as "Father", and he encouraged his followers to do the same, which would seem to make us *all* sons or daughters of God, in some sense (*John* 1:12 and *Romans* 8:14-17). But Jesus had also been described by New Testament writers as *the* Son of God, in a unique sense. The debate at Nicea focused on the question whether Jesus was of a lesser or the same status as God the Father, and the latter view was decisively accepted by the Council.

It was thus confirmed that the fundamental dogma of Christianity was to be that Jesus was both fully divine and fully human—a claim that is blasphemous to Jews and Muslims. For Christians, the coming of Jesus had changed their conception of God, and this was not merely by *adding* something to what the Jews already believed, for a God who could become incarnate in a human being is a different sort of God from the Yahweh of the Old Testament. It is a nice question whether the Church would have fixated on the literal divinity of Christ if Constantine had not used his imperial power to secure agreement at Nicea. However such historical hypotheticals are not usually answerable: Christian theologians may say that God used Constantine as his instrument to guide the Church into truth, but they can be challenged to say whether God has equally guided the Papacy, Eastern Orthodoxy, and the Reformers (who cannot all be right). Others will wonder about the element of historical contingency in the development of theology.

The Trinity, the Holy Spirit, and Eastern Orthodox Christianity

The distinctively Christian Trinitarian conception of God as Father, Son, and Holy Spirit was not fully developed until after the Council of Nicea. There was considerable talk of God's spirit in the Old Testament, and Paul had written that "in each of us the Spirit is seen to be at work for some useful purpose" (*1 Corinthians* 12), and "God has given the Spirit to dwell in our hearts" (*2 Corinthians* 1:22). The implication seems to be that there is something divine within human beings generally, not just Jesus. The question arose what relation this "Holy Spirit" bears to God the Father, and to Christ. The 4th-century Church was persuaded at successive Councils that the Spirit had to be recognized as a third aspect of God, and this was expressed in the paradoxical formula "three persons in one God". This does not mean that Christians believed in three gods (as Jews or Muslims may allege), but in three aspects of God, or three ways of experiencing God.

Theologians tend to admit, though, that the Holy Spirit has been the "Cinderella" of the Trinity, getting less attention than the other two members. The creeds start with God as Creator and go on to say a great deal about Jesus, but they only mention the Holy Spirit (or "Holy Ghost") in one sentence, like an afterthought. Christian evangelists proclaim that Jesus was the Son of God, but they are less often heard saying that the Holy Spirit is equally divine. Yet in the order of actual human experience, the Spirit may be thought to be the aspect of God that we can most readily experience. If we are fortunate, we may recognize in some of the people we meet such virtues and graces that deserve to be called gifts of the Spirit:

> The harvest of the Spirit is love, joy, peace, patience, kindness, goodness, fidelity, gentleness, and self-control. (*Galatians* 5:22-3)

If we are *very* fortunate, we might even experience something of this within ourselves, though any claim to do so had better be very cautiously and humbly expressed! Many famous Christians (such as St. Augustine, and George Fox, for whom see Chapter 6) have said that we can each have experience of God within ourselves; but they also talk of experiencing the *Spirit* of God or the *Spirit* of Christ—and aren't these alternative phrases for the same thing?

Trinitarian theology was involved in one of the biggest schisms within Christendom, but to explain this we have to go back to another epoch-making decision of the Emperor Constantine. In 330 he founded a new Eastern capital for the Roman Empire on the Bosporus, where Europe confronts Asia across that narrow stretch of water, and in his honour the new city was named Constantinople (now Istanbul). Soon afterwards the unmanageable Empire divided into two parts, and in the 5th century Rome fell to the invading barbarians, though the Bishop of Rome became the leader of Western Christians and acquired the title of "Pope". But the Eastern, Greek-speaking portion of the Roman empire lived on as "the Second Rome" for another millennium until its conquest by the Turks in 1453; it became known as Byzantium.

The Greek- and Latin-speaking traditions within Christianity started to diverge, especially on how to interpret the doctrine of the Trinity. As time went on the Byzantines evolved a different form of Christianity now known as Eastern Orthodoxy. There was a formal separation in 1054, offically over the extremely arcane matter of whether the Nicene Creed should be amended to say that the Holy Spirit "proceeds from the Father and the Son (*filioque*)", or just "from the Father". Ever since then, the two traditions have been sharply distinct. Indeed, they came to blows in 1204 when the Crusaders from Western Europe who had been mobilized by the Pope to try to expel the Muslims from the Holy Land called in at Constantinople on their way to Jerusalem. It was not a friendly visit, however, for the army of supposedly Christian knights sacked the city, despite its being the centre of a Christian civilization. This was not the first or last time that theological differences have been associated with violence.

The development of Christian theology has produced a remarkably elaborate intellectual edifice—or rather, a number of competing theories which differ on seemingly obscure points. One has to ask what was (and is) really at stake in these debates? Is it just a matter of party-spirit, each expressing loyalty to their revered predecessors? Or is there some criterion of truth in theology, some way of deciding which view is right, at least provisionally? Modern science gets highly technical and mathematical, and it tells us about things that are way beyond the reach of our unaided sense-perception. But scientific theories eventually have to be testable, however indirectly, by some sort of observation, nowadays often involving elaborate instrumentation. By appealing to observed evidence, scientists have been able to reach a remarkable degree of worldwide, culture-independent, agreement on most points. But this has not applied to theological differences, whether between religions, or rival versions of one religion: it does not seem that there has been any agreed progress in theology.

If there is anything that deserves to be recognized as a criterion of theological truth, it surely must have to do with what can make us better people. The exact meaning or standard of "better" remains to be explored, and there may be different conceptions of "salvation" on offer, but the basic core of virtue is plainly given by Paul's words in *Galatians* quoted above. Thus the mysterious theological or metaphysical claims about God, Christ, and Holy Spirit had better be referred back to human experience. But that does not mean that we should each decide for ourselves, in the light of our own limited and idiosyncratic experience. We can each learn from the experience of others, not just in our own time, but down the centuries. One important place to look is of course the New Testament, where there are some striking expressions of experience "of the Spirit", for example:

> To prove that you are sons, God has sent into our hearts the Spirit of his Son, crying "Abba, Father!" (*Galatians* 4:6)

> For it is by the Spirit and through faith that we hope to attain that righteousness which we eagerly await. (*Galatians* 5:5)

> But when the kindness and generosity of God our Saviour dawned upon the world, then, not for any good deeds of our own, but because he was merciful, he saved us though the water of rebirth and the renewing power of the Holy Spirit ... (*Titus* 3:4–5)

But if these words are to be not just pious phrases, we have to be convinced that they can refer to something in our own experience. I will return to this in introducing the Quaker movement in Chapter 6.

To conclude this section, let us note that Orthodox Christianity was adopted in a top-down decision by the 10th-century rulers of Rus, the small seed from which the huge nation of modern Russia has grown. After the Turkish conquest of Constantinople, Russian Orthodox Christianity liked to entitle itself "the Third Rome", claiming to carry the true heritage of ancient Christianity. Orthodoxy continues to this day in Greece and Eastern Europe, and it is resurgent in Russia after severe persecution in the communist era. It should also be remembered that there are other forms of Christianity with very ancient roots which are neither Orthodox nor Catholic—such as the Coptic churches of Egypt and Ethiopia, and the very early Christian church in South India.

Muhammad and the birth of Islam

Mention of the anti-Islamic Crusaders and the Muslim Turks prompts us to go back to the origins of Islam. This new religion erupted like a volcano out of the Arabian peninsula in the 7th century CE, but it did not come out of nothing. The pre-Islamic Arabs thought of themselves as having a common Semitic ancestry with the Jews from the patriarch Abraham and his first son Ishmael, and they already had the Ka'ba in Mecca as their central focus of polytheistic worship. There had long been Jews and Zoroastrians in Arabia, and more recently there were Christians, so it was a multi-religious society into which the prophet Muhammad (570–632) was born.

Like Jesus before him Muhammad did not intend to found a new religion, but to reform Arabian beliefs and practices in the name of the monotheistic God of Judaism and Christianity:

> In matters of faith, He has laid down for you [people] the same commandment that he gave Noah, which We have revealed to you [Muhammad] and which We enjoined on Abraham and Moses and Jesus ... (*Qur'an* 42.13)

The *Qur'an* makes repeated respectful references to the Hebrew patriarchs, and to Jesus and his mother Mary (though not to Old Testament prophets such as Isaiah or Jeremiah, or to any of the New Testament writers). Muhammad clearly thought he was worshipping the same God as the Jews and the Christians. The *Qur'an* describes them as "People of the Book" and claims to be adding to the revelations already received:

> We have sent revelations to you [Prophet] as We did to Noah and the prophets after him, to Abraham, Ishmael, Isaac, Jacob, and the Tribes, to Jesus, Job, Jonah, Aaron and Solomon—to David We gave the book [of *Psalms*] ... (*Qur'an* 4:163)

Muhammad's home town of Mecca was ruled by the powerful Quraysh tribe, who controlled the trading routes. He rose in status by marrying a wealthy widow, but he developed doubts about his involvement in economic exploitation, and started going on spiritual retreats and giving to the poor. In the year 610, he had the first of a series of dreams or visions in which, he claimed, he was given direct revelations from

God. Over the next twenty years or so, he received a stream of such verbal revelations (in Arabic, of course) which he apparently memorized. When compiled after his death, these became the text of the *Qur'an*. Islam thus resembles Judaism and Christianity in believing that a certain set of writings are the revealed Word of God. But unlike the Old and New Testaments, the *Qur'an* originated through one man only, who claimed to have received it dictated directly by God, word for word. Islam therefore takes the divine nature of its sacred text even more literally than Judaism and Christianity. In the Arabic, the *Qur'an* has an exquisite poetic quality which has obviously contributed to its appeal, especially to a pre-literate people for whom oral recitation was vital. The poetry does not survive so well in translation, but the non-Arabic speaker can experience something of it when hearing it sung in haunting musical tones.

The message given to Muhammad was both theological and social. It strongly emphasized the unity and sovereignty and love of God, the Creator of all things. Almost every *sura* (chapter) of the *Qur'an* has the heading: "In the name of God, the Lord of Mercy, the Giver of Mercy". And, in words strikingly reminiscent of the later Hebrew prophets and the sayings of Jesus, it commands compassion for the underprivileged and the oppressed, and sternly warns the wealthy:

> So do not be harsh with the orphan and do not chide the one who asks for help; talk about the blessings of your Lord. (*Qur'an* 93:9–11)

> Woe to every fault-finding backbiter who amasses riches, counting them over, thinking they will make him live for ever. No indeed! He will be thrust into the Crusher! What will explain to you what the Crusher is? It is God's fire, made to blaze, which rises over people's hearts. (*Qur'an* 104:1–7)

It can surely be concluded that the twin commandment to love God and love one's neighbour is central to Islam as well as to Judaism and Christianity.

This radical message was a threat to the wealth and power of the Quraysh in Mecca, and they offered Muhammad inducements to cease preaching. When he refused, they tried to cut off his income, and when he lost the protection of some powerful individuals in Meccan society, he and his followers fled to Yathrib some two hundred miles to the north, which he renamed Medina. Medina was the real originating place of Islam, for it was in this obscure desert oasis that a new kind of society — the Muslim *umma* — was born, and Muhammad's Arab reform movement developed into a universal religious ideology. Muslims of many different tendencies thus tend to look back to Medina as the paradigm of Islam.

To begin with, Muhammad may have been seen only as a tribal leader, although to his followers he was already a divinely-appointed prophet and lawgiver. But his role soon outgrew the traditional tribal model. Membership of the new community was opened to anyone who would declare "There is no god but God, and Muhammad is God's Messenger" — which is still the basic test for conversion to Islam. That brief second clause has enormous implications, for it makes Muhammad much more than an Arab sheikh, more indeed than one more prophet to add to the list, for it is implied that he is "the Seal" (i.e. the last) of the prophets, i.e. that the revelations of God have been completed through him. (But dare one ask: how is one supposed to know that revelation stopped in the 7th century — has God nothing left to say?)

Muhammad laid down a new spiritually-based ethic which reformed the old Arab ways, in partial parallel with Jesus's revitalization of the Old Testament commandments. He affirmed the principle of proportionate retribution for wrong, but praised forgiveness as better:

> Let harm be requited by an equal harm, though anyone who forgives and puts things right will have his reward from God — He does not like those who do wrong. There is no cause to act against anyone who defends himself after being wronged, but there is cause to act against those who oppress people and transgress in the land against all justice — they will have an agonizing torment — though if a person is patient and forgives, this is one of the greatest things. (*Qur'an* 42:40–43)

In Medina, Muhammad proclaimed the equal worth of all members of the *umma* regardless of class or wealth — including women, as the *Qur'an* says at 33:35, though men and women take on different roles in society (4:34). He limited the number of wives a man could take, and gave women a right to divorce their husbands. It will surprise many to know that the veil is not explicitly enjoined on women in the *Qur'an*. On this and on many other points, it remains a matter of dispute within Islam as to what is actually said or implied by the *Qu'ran* and what is only a matter of changeable cultural practice. (Similar questions arise within Christianity and Judaism.) Muhammad instituted a tax (the

RATIONALISM OR FUNDAMENTALISM

zakat) to be distributed to the neediest members of the community; and this remains one of the compulsory features of Islam:

> The truly good are those who believe in God and the Last Day, in the angels, the Scripture, and the prophets; who give away some of their wealth, however much they cherish it, to their relatives, to orphans, the needy, travelers and beggars, and to liberate those in bondage ... (*Qur'an* 2:177)

The Quraysh of Mecca tried to wipe out this radical new ideology and community by armed force. Unlike Jesus, Muhammad led his soldiers on the field of battle, and narrowly avoided being killed. But contrary both to Western perceptions from the Crusades onwards and to present-day terrorist perversions, the Islamic concept of *jihad* means primarily the spiritual struggle between good and evil within the individual, and only secondarily the waging of war. After a few years of conflict with the Quraysh, Muhammad led his people unopposed into Mecca in 630, where he cleansed the Ka'ba of its pagan idols and rededicated it as the centre of Muslim pilgrimage (the *hajj*) which it has been ever since. Two years later he died.

Medieval Islam

The death of Muhammad left the new Muslim community unprepared, without any guidance about who should lead it. The *Qur'an* had not yet been compiled, and people appealed to *hadith*, alleged sayings of the Prophet, whose authenticity was often in dispute. Factional conflict arose, and two of the first four Caliphs were killed. It was unclear from the start whether the position of "Caliph", i.e. the political leadership of the *umma*, should also carry religious authority. After the murders of the fourth Caliph Ali, who was cousin and son-in-law of Muhammad, and of his son Huysan in 680 at Karbala (now in Iraq), there arose a deep schism between Sunni and Shi'ite Muslims which has continued to the present day. The Shi'ites held that the leader or *"imam"* should have come from Muhammad's family line, and they still look for a divinely-inspired imam to continue the prophetic tradition. Iranians and many Iraqis remain Shi'ite, but the majority of world Muslims are Sunnis, and Shi'ites tend to feel a historic sense of injustice.

The sudden growth of Islam generated a dynamic force in the hitherto backward region of desert nomads in Arabia. The experience of internal conflict seem to have given the Arabs a taste for military victory in the name of religion, and they soon started exporting their armies and their Islamic rule to their neighbours. Within a century, Islam had conquered the Middle East, North Africa and Spain, and as far East as the gates of India. The high-water mark of the advance of Muslim armies into Western Europe was only a few miles from Paris, where they were defeated in 732. The Caliphate of the 8th century (ruled from Baghdad) rivaled the Roman Empire in extent, though it did not include Turkey, Greece or Italy.

From the 8th to the 12th centuries there was a great flowering of Islamic culture, which was then one of the great civilizations of the world. In Syria, Muslim scholars found Greek texts preserved from the ancient world, and translated them into Arabic. Amongst them were the lost scientific and philosophical works of Aristotle. Islamic thinkers started to develop intellectual systems that tried to combine Greek philosophy (mainly Aristotelianism and neo-Platonism) with the Islamic faith. In this Islamic "Golden Age", theology, philosophy, science and medicine were far more advanced than in Western Europe, which was still struggling to emerge from the "Dark Ages" that followed the fall of the Roman Empire.

From the start of Islam, theological authority tended to pass to the *ulama*, the Islamic religious scholars, who have been entirely male and usually very conservative. For better or for worse they have retained their authority down to the present day, though like theologians of other faiths they tend to be divided amongst themselves. Islamic thought resembles Judaism and Christianity in assuming as an unquestionable premise the authority of a religious tradition based on an allegedly divine revelation. But in those five centuries of classic Islamic civilization there emerged some hotly debated differences about the relation of reason to faith, and of individual religious experience to religious authority.

As well as philosophical theology there developed an influential tradition of Islamic piety and mysticism in the Sufi movement, which still continues in various Sufi brotherhoods (which might be partially compared to Christian monastic orders). For Muslim mystics, true piety means finding God's beauty revealed in everything in the world, and our deepest yearnings are fulfilled in ever-greater intimacy with God. But Sufism was often regarded with suspicion by the *ulama*, and in the 10th century al-Hallaj was executed for publicly proclaiming his claim to have achieved mystical union with God. Yet in the 13th century Rumi was writing mystical poetry that echoes the *Song of Songs* in the

Old Testament and the *Confessions* of St. Augustine, and has had an appeal well beyond Islam:

> I am bewildered by the Beloved,
> He belongs to me.
> Do not search elsewhere;
> He lives in my heart.
> I am not misleading you when I say
> I am Him!

One of the deepest Islamic rationalist thinkers was ibn Sina (980–1037), whose name was latinized in the West as 'Avicenna'. He was expert in medicine and philosophy, mathematics and theology, and is credited with a hundred books—including twenty recipes for contraceptives! Deeply influenced by Aristotle, Ibn Sina tended to treat all questions about the world by reason alone, without appeal to the *Qur'an*. In theology, he offered a theory of "prophecy" or revelation according to which God spoke through the divine intellect in the mind of Muhammad, whereas the imaginative side of the prophet's mind expressed religious truths in terms of vivid images and parables. Such imagery is usually needed to persuade unthinking people and impel them to action, but according to ibn Sina philosophers can reinterpret the images in terms of higher spiritual truths, and those who worship God in purely spiritual love are the highest of mankind. He also expressed doubts about the literal truth of bodily resurrection. (I will be addressing similar themes for myself in Chapters 9 and 10.)

But in Islam as in other religions there was typically a reaction by traditionalist or fundamentalist believers and scholars against such rationalist or supposedly "enlightened" thinking. Muslim rationalists said that theological arguments and Qur'anic interpretation must conform to the principles of human reason; and one Caliph even made an ill-advised attempt to enforce rationalism on the *ulama*, using a system of inquisition. But more traditional scholars continued to insist that reason must be subordinate to revelation, that the *Qur'an* must be interpreted literally, and even that Muslims must "believe without asking why" (like Tertullian in early Christianity). They found an influential ally in Al-Ghazali, a brilliant scholar who gave up his professorship in Baghdad for the life of a wandering ascetic and Sufi. In a book aggressively entitled *The Incoherence of the Philosophers* he criticized Islamic philosophers for being over-influenced by Greek ideas and departing from Qur'anic orthodoxy. He defended the Islamic conception of God as wholly indivisible, unique and indefinable:

"Nothing is like Him, and He is not like anything", so human language can only speak of Him in symbols and metaphors. Al-Ghazali tended to appeal to religious experience rather than philosophical argument, but even he reacted against the stultification of thought by the increasingly conservative *ulama*.

By the 13th century, traditionalism had become dominant in Sunni Islam, and many rationalist thinkers were being branded as heretics. In Spain there was a last-ditch defence of philosophy by ibn Rushd (1126-1198, Latin name: "Averroes") who lived in Cordoba in the Islamic state of *el-Andalus* (now Andalusia). He argued that since the text of the *Qu'ran* often needs interpretation, and its interpreters disagree on questions of law and ethics, Muslims cannot avoid the use of reason. He wrote a reply to al-Ghazali entitled *The Incoherence of "The Incoherence"*, arguing that it was inconsistent to use reason to argue against reliance on reason. He too defended a two-level theory of knowledge, in which philosophy establishes the literal truth about reality using human reason, while popular religion offers a simplified version for the masses, using signs and symbols, poetry and metaphorical language. Although he was careful to add that the mature philosopher will neither utter nor encourage any word against the established faith, ibn Rushd's rationalist Aristotelian approach to theology was anathema to the traditional scholars. In 1150 the Caliph had ordered the burning of ibn Sina's philosophical works; in 1194 those of ibn Rushd suffered the same fate, and at the end of his life he was banished from his native city of Cordoba.

From the 13th century until recently, mainstream Islam largely turned its back on independent scientific, philosophical and theological thought, in which for some centuries it had led the world. The fundamentalist appeal to the Qu'ranic revelation and the Sufi emphasis on religious experience remained more important than rational theology or scholarly legalism in the piety of most Muslims. Much of their devotion has been focused on the figure of Muhammad. Officially Islam insists that he was only a human Messenger of God's final revelation, not an incarnation of God Himself—as Christianity has traditionally claimed about Jesus. But popular Muslim devotion, especially under Sufi influence, has tended to see Muhammad in cosmic terms as a perfect human being, a worker of miracles, a flawless and infallible messenger and interpreter of God's will who was blessed by ascension to heaven, and remains as the goal of all mystical seekers of the truth. Around the Muslim world, celebrations of Muhammad's birthday (the *Mawlid*) rival the Christian Christmas. One of the liturgies used by Sufi orders uses the 13th century *Poem of the Cloak* in praise of Muhammad:

> Lofty mountains of gold were brought to tempt him
> Away from himself. But he turned away however high they might be.
> His earthly needs only strengthened his pious austerity in the face of such temptations.
> For truly need never prevails over the infallible.
> How can worldly necessities incline such a noble personality towards this earthly life,
> When if not for him this world would not have been brought out of non-existence.
>
> Refrain: O my Lord, send your peace and blessings always and forever,
> Upon your Beloved (Muhammad), the best of all creation.

No doubt much of the poetic quality is lost in translation, but there are obvious parallels with Christian devotion to Jesus—his rejection of worldly temptations (*Matthew* 4:1–11), the ascription to him of infallibility (*John* 14:6), and of a cosmic role in the very creation and redemption of the world (*John* 8:58, *Colossians* 1:13–20).

Medieval Judaism

It is ironic that two of the greatest thinkers of medieval Islam, Ibn Sina and Ibn Rushd, had more influence on Western thought than on their own religion, by passing the torch of rediscovered Aristotelian philosophy to Christianity and Judaism. In the introduction to Chapter 3 I sketched the history of the Jews up to the time of Jesus. After the sack of Jerusalem by the Romans in 70 CE, and their defeat of another Jewish rebellion in 135 CE, the Jews dispersed over many lands, and their religion changed and developed as it became centred on synagogues and rabbis instead of the destroyed Temple. Over the first centuries CE, various rabbis compiled the *Talmud*, a vast rambling encyclopedia of Jewish history, theology, ritual, medicine, folklore, property, commerce and law. This became almost as central to the Jewish identity as the Torah itself (the first five books of the Hebrew Bible). The role of the *Talmud* could even be compared to that of the New Testament for Christians, and it has been remarked that it functioned for Jews in their dispersed communities as a portable Fatherland.

But in the 8th century there was a fundamentalist reaction. The "Karaites" urged Jews to reject the accumulated rabbinical teachings in the *Talmud*, and go back to the Torah as the only authoritative source of God's revelation. Their leader Anan praised Jesus as a holy man who had not intended to set aside the ancient Jewish Law or to found a new religion, but rather to cleanse and reform Judaism. In the 9th century some Karaites abandoned Anan's principle of literal interpretation, and suggested that physical descriptions of God and bodily resurrection should be understood metaphorically. But the more orthodox rabbis reverted to literalism: apparently some of them even offered to estimate the measurements of God's body and beard! Saadia (892–942) offered a carefully-argued compromise which tried to reconcile tradition both with the original texts and with human rationality. He proposed that where the Bible contradicts reason, we may take it that the passage is not meant to be interpreted literally by adult minds. (We have found similar suggestions within Christianity and Islam.)

In medieval Europe, Jews were sometimes tolerated but at other times persecuted. As a persistent minority maintaining a stubbornly different non-Christian identity (shown in diet and often in clothing), they were always seen as strangers within the gates. They were found financially useful, however, because their religion allowed them to lend money at interest—a practice which traditional Christianity condemned as "usury" (though it has long since come to terms with it, for better or for worse!) But there was a depressing series of pogroms and expulsions, notably when the crusaders started off their Papally-blessed march to the Holy Land by massacring Jews in the Rhineland. In Islamic Spain Jews enjoyed better treatment for the most part, and some were appointed to high office.

The greatest medieval Jewish philosopher was Maimonides, affectionately known as "Rambam" (1135–1204). He was born in Cordoba a few years after Ibn Rushd, but those two great thinkers of different religions never met, for Maimonides had to leave when Berber fanatics took over the city and expelled Jews and Christians. He ended up in Cairo, where he became physician to the Muslim rulers, and wrote ten medical books in Arabic. His best-known work is the *Guide for the Perplexed*, in which he tried to reconcile Aristotelian philosophy with rabbinic teaching. The perplexity he aimed to assuage is not that of the uncommitted inquirer wondering which religion to accept, but rather that of the pious Jew who finds some passages of the Hebrew Bible apparently repugnant to reason. Like Saadia (and Origen, Ibn

Sina, Ibn Rushd, and many others) Maimonides suggested a two-level theory of religious truth:

> Our sages have said, It is impossible to give a full account of the creation to man. ... It has been treated in metaphors in order that the uneducated may comprehend it according to the measure of their faculties and the feebleness of their apprehension, while educated people may take it in a different sense. (*Guide for the Perplexed* I, introduction)

And he offered his own version of "apophatic" theology:

> You should know that God (may He be exalted and praised!) can only correctly be described by negative attributes. A negative description is not tainted by fanciful exaggeration and does not imply that God is deficient in any general or particular way. ... I will show that we are not able to describe him in any way except by describing what he is not. (*Guide for the Perplexed* I)

Yet Maimonides was sternly orthodox in insisting that Jews do know (very positively!) that every word in the Pentateuch is divinely inspired, and that any Jew who repudiated the Law should be put to death. However he was very radical about the afterlife: he followed Ibn Rushd's denial of individual immortality, and interpreted the doctrine of resurrection of the body as a mere concession to the imaginative needs of the populace.

Inevitably, there was a traditionalist reaction. Many rabbis fought back against what they contemptuously described as "selling the Scriptures to the Greeks", and they condemned the conception of "the unknowable God" as destructive of true religion and piety. His tomb was desecrated, and some Jewish zealots denounced his books to the Dominican Inquisition as containing heresies dangerous to Christianity as well as Judaism! Jewish medieval philosophy thus suffered something of the same fate as its Islamic version, namely being overrun by religious tradition and enthusiastic fundamentalism.

As in Christianity and Islam, there was a mystical element in Jewish piety that developed strongly in the later middle ages, and had more popular influence than rational philosophy. The mystical theological and spiritual tradition of the Kabbalah gained a place in Judaism akin to that of Sufism in Islam. It is represented in the 13th century *Hymn of Glory* that still has an honoured place in Jewish liturgy:

> Songs I weave and tunes I utter, for my soul doth pant for thee.
> Longing in thy powerful shade to know thy secret mystery.

> As thy glory I describe, my mind suspires to soar above,
> So I sing about thy glory, glorifying thy name with love.
>
> All unseeing I sing thy glory, all unknowing I speak of thee
> By thy faithful prophets showing images of mystery.
> Calling on thy works they named thee, picturing thy power and might;
> Drawing on thy deeds they framed thee, who wert hidden from their sight.
> Every vision paints its picture, but in essence thou art One.
> Fully of years or youthful victor, flushed with pride of battles won.

Such expression of direct relationship to God—without any intermediary like Jesus or Mary, or Muhammad—is typical of Jewish spirituality going back to the Psalms. In the late middle ages it was remarkably developed in the Lurianic Kabbalah, and in later centuries it flowed into the influential Jewish pietist movement known as Hasidism.

It is a remarkable fact that in the 12th and 13th centuries there was a three-way debate between Christian, Islamic and Jewish thinkers in Muslim Andalusia. But this brief era of multiculturalism was not to last: with the gradual reconquest of the Iberian peninsula by the Spanish Catholic Kings intolerance and conflict took over, and after the final capture of Granada in 1492 Jews and Muslims were expelled. Thus at the Western end of the Mediterranean militant Catholicism ejected Islam and Judaism, while at the Eastern end the Muslim Turks ended the thousand years of Byzantium when Constantinople fell to them in 1453.

Christian scholastic philosophy

In the "high middle ages" of the 12th and 13th centuries France and England became prosperous and powerful. Soaring gothic cathedrals were built, there was a revival of culture and scholarship, and universities were founded. It is conventional to describe this as "the age of faith", yet there was a surprising amount of independent thought, and some debate with Jewish and Muslim philosophers. A variety of unorthodoxies and heresies grew up, and the Catholic Church founded the Inquisition to combat them by excommunication, torture and burnings at the stake. One of the largest groups were the Cathars or Albigensians in southern France, but a ruthless policy of spiritual and physical extermination was used to suppress them and establish the central power of the new French state.

The newly-established universities, especially in Paris, became a hotbed of intellectual debate, and talented students came from all over Europe to sit at the feet of the greatest thinkers of the time. Pierre Abelard (1079–1142) became a superstar for his philosophy and his stylish way with words — and for his notorious love-affair with Heloise, for which her relations took cruel revenge by castrating him. He was over-confident in his thinking too, and he soon aroused the suspicion of more conservative forces by his approach to theology. In his *Dialogue between a Philosopher, a Jew, and a Christian* the philosopher boldly asserted that it is absurd to cling to the beliefs of childhood, to share the superstitions of the crowd, and to condemn to hell those who do not share them — a dangerous declaration of intellectual independence! Abelard's famous work *Yes and No* offered arguments for and against 157 "Questions", amongst them the fundamental dogmas of the Christian faith. In the prologue he invited trouble by writing:

> The first key to wisdom is assiduous and frequent questioning ... For by doubting we come to inquiry, and by inquiry we arrive at the truth.

Clerics became nervous about the influence such a freethinking approach was having on excitable young minds, and Abelard was indicted for heresy, for his interpretation of the Trinity. The offending book was burnt, and he was sent to a monastery, but he still continued to attract students and to write books that were deemed dangerous. Eventually the conservatives called in their heaviest weapon, the saintly but stern Bernard of Clairvaux, head of the Cistercian monastic order, who presided at a council meeting that condemned sixteen propositions from Abelard's writings. At the age of 63, Abelard set out for Rome to appeal to the Pope, but died on the way.

Despite this setback, philosophy was to achieve a more secure home in Christianity than it did in Islam or Judaism. As we saw in the previous chapter, much Christian theology had made use of Platonic Greek philosophy from its beginnings. But the works of Aristotle did not become available to the West until the 12th century, when they were rediscovered from the Arabs. At first the Church tried to stop this influx of new philosophical thought, but the influence of Aristotle and his able Muslim commentator Ibn Rushd grew.

St. Thomas Aquinas (1224–1274) came to dominate the end of the Christian middle ages, by harmonizing Aristotle's philosophy with Christian theology in his 21-volume *Summa Theologica*. In calm and measured tones he carefully presents arguments for and against each question that he raises, but unlike Abelard he always comes firmly down on the side of orthodoxy. He allowed that the powers of human reason have a legitimate though limited place in the defence of Christian faith. In rational theology, we can use human reason to prove the existence of God (by the "Five Ways" presented in the *Summa*); in revealed theology, we must receive in faith the revelation of God's nature through the Bible and the Church, though we can and should use our reason to elucidate its content.

On human nature, Aquinas followed an Aristotelian analysis of our "rational soul" as consisting in our capacities for perception, intellectual conception, theoretical reasoning, practical deliberation and free decision. But to provide for the afterlife, he retained (with dubious consistency) an element of Platonic dualism, saying that although the resurrection involves the recreation of the complete human being as a union of body and soul, the soul has a disembodied existence in between death and resurrection. In that way he tried to maintain personal identity into the afterlife—but it remains unclear how a disembodied soul can be a perceiving and acting person.

Aquinas's appeal to reason was real, but limited. The authority of the Catholic Church remained paramount for him in all matters of faith, and where Aristotle differs from Christian doctrine, the latter prevails. Like most medievals, Aquinas was prepared to sanction the use of force against dissent, and said that heretics who produce perversions of the Christian faith may be "banished from the world by death" (II-II, Q.11, art 3). His great intellectual synthesis was constructed for the glory of God, but also to buttress the authority of the Church—and in some of its darker corners a whiff of burning can still be smelt. He did not quite finish his vast intellectual construction, for in the last year of his life he apparently experienced a mystical vision, and said that all he had written "seemed to him as straw". The *Summa* is like a medieval cathedral: an enormous, impressive structure of high religious aspiration, full of intricate detail which makes one marvel at the faith and the workmanship that produced it. Though controversial in its own time, it has since become Roman Catholic orthodoxy.

In this chapter we have seen how in the three semitic religions both religious experience and philosophical thought have led to clashes with traditional religious authorities and their power-structures. The tension between individual experience and appeal to scriptural revelation, and between rationalist and fundamentalist tendencies, has been characteristic of all three religions—and we can find it resurfacing in every generation down to the present. Late medieval Christianity made a somewhat uneasy peace with philosophy, but Islam and Judaism did not, despite being shown the way by some of their ablest thinkers.

Further reading

Will Durant, *The Story of Civilization: Part IV: The Age of Faith* (New York, Simon and Schuster 1950)

In *The Bible: The Biography* (London: Atlantic Books 2007), Karen Armstrong explores how that very mixed compilation of writings known as the Bible has been formed, interpreted and misinterpreted down the ages.

In Oxford University Press's Very Short Introduction series, there are books on *The Bible* by John Riches, on *Paul* by E.P. Sanders, on *Augustine* by Henry Chadwick, on *Thomas Aquinas* by Fergus Kerr, on *Christianity* by Linda Woodhead, and on *Theology* by David F. Ford. A longer work is Alister E. McGrath, *Christian Theology: An Introduction* (Oxford: Blackwell, 3rd edition 2001)

The Qur'an, translated by M.A.S. Abdel Haleem (Oxford: Oxford University Press 2004)

In Oxford University Press's Very Short Introduction series, there are books on *Muhammad* by Jonathan A.C. Brown (2011), on *The Koran* by Michael Cook (2000), on *Islam* by Malise Ruthven (2000), on *Islamic History* by Adam J. Silverstein (2010).

Reza Aslan, *There is no god but God: The Origins, Evolution and Future of Islam* (London: Arrow Books 2006)

Rumi: Gardens of the Beloved, translated by Mayam Mafi and Azima Mdelita Kolin (London: Element 2003)

Nicolas de Lange, *Judaism* (Oxford: Oxford University Press 1986)

Lavinia and Dan Cohn-Sherbok, *Judaism: A Short Reader* (Oxford: Oneworld Publications 1996)

Norman Solomon, *Judaism* (2000), and Joseph Dan, *Kabbalah*, in Oxford University Press's Very Short Introduction series.

Malise Ruthven, *Fundamentalism*, in Oxford University Press's Very Short Introduction series.

CHAPTER 6

GEORGE FOX AND THE BEGINNING OF THE QUAKERS

The Reformation

Four intellectual movements of world-historical importance developed in early modern Europe—the Renaissance, the Reformation, the Rise of Science, and the Enlightenment. In the Renaissance in the 15th and 16th centuries, new attention was devoted to the literature, arts and philosophy of the ancient world, and there arose a more human-centred or humanist style of thinking that was independent of Christianity though still respectful of it. In the great flowering of Italian painting and sculpture interest focused on the human form, though the subject-matter usually remained nominally religious. The plays of Shakespeare, several of them set in Roman times, have human nature and motivation as their central theme.

The Reformation is usually reckoned to have begun when Martin Luther nailed ninety-five controversial theses challenging papal authority on a church door in Wittenberg in Germany in 1517. Luther (1483-1546) was a monk in the Augustinian order, and also a professor of theology in the newly-founded university of Wittenberg where he lectured on the philosophy of Aristotle as well as on the Bible. He felt led to question some of the practices of the Catholic Church, and he was especially provoked by the sale of "indulgences", in which people were given to believe that they could buy forgiveness and a place in heaven by contributing funds to the Church (especially for the magnificent rebuilding of St. Peter's in Rome). More fundamentally, Luther had found himself tortured by a strong sense of sin and recurring doubt about how he could become acceptable in the sight of

God, and the most distinctive theme of his theology was that we human sinners are forgiven by God according to his freely-given grace, not for our good behaviour (though that should follow). This "justification" in the sight of God depends entirely on our individual responses of faith, not the mediation of the Church; nor does it depend on our human rationality, for Luther notoriously dismissed reason as a "whore", believing that we tend to pervert our intelligence to sinful ends. He summed up his message of Christian freedom in the following idealistic passage:

> I have taught in such a way that my teaching would lead first and foremost to a knowledge of Christ, that is, to pure and proper faith and genuine love, and thereby to freedom in all matters of external conduct such as eating, drinking, clothes, praying, fasting, monasteries, sacrament, and whatever it may be. Such freedom is used in a salutary way only by those who have faith and love, that is, those who are real Christians. On such people we can and should impose no human law — not permit anyone else to do so — which would bind their conscience.

George Fox and modern-day Quakers would, I think, agree — as we shall see.

Luther was something of a German nationalist, reacting against the power of Rome, and it was crucial that he was given protection by some of the rulers of small German princely states, otherwise his excommunication would almost certainly have been followed by burning. Using his knowledge of Hebrew and Greek, he translated the Bible into German; and such translations into the vernacular languages of the people became a crucial element of the new Protestant spirituality. Until then, the Bible had been available only to priests and theologians, but now appeal to Scripture became the fundamental source of authority for Protestants.

The Lutheran reform movement soon split into different parties who wanted to change faster, or slower, than Luther himself. In Switzerland, Zwingli and Calvin (1509–1564) differed from him about the interpretation of the eucharist, for he still insisted that in some sense Christ was really present in the bread and wine while they said the sacrament was merely symbolic. Calvinism, also known as "Reformed" Christianity, inspired the mid-16th century reformation in Scotland, it influenced the Puritan movement in England, and hence the early colonies in North America. There developed a Protestant doctrine of the infallibility of the Bible as the revealed word of God: but devout readers often disagree about how to interpret its texts, so the question of who has the correct interpretation always tends to arise, and thus sects have diverged and multiplied. Some of the more radical Protestants such as the Anabaptists on the Continent (who rejected the practice of infant baptism, and insisted on adult commitment instead) and the Quakers in England (whom we are about to examine in detail) appealed to "the inner Light" of God's revelation in the individual mind or heart, at least as much as to Scripture — but of course that is even more subject to individual interpretation.

The movement of religious reform that Luther started spread rapidly across Europe. The unity of the Western Church was shattered, and there arose bitter and often violent struggles between Catholics and Protestants for control of towns, regions, and whole nations. After the 16th- and 17th-century wars of religion, which included a good deal of what we would now call ethnic "cleansing", Europe ended up with nation-states that were largely uniform in religion: France and Spain as the main Catholic powers, and most of northern Europe being Protestant (with Poland and Ireland as exceptions), and Germany remaining a patchwork of Catholic and Protestant. This identification of different versions of Christianity with national identities has lasted into our own time, but is now eroding under secularization.

17th-century England

The early Quakers, who might be described as part of a third phase of the Reformation, claimed to be returning to primitive Christianity, but to understand them we need to know something of what led up to the troubled 17th century in Britain. In England the Reformation had followed a top-down, zigzag course under successive Tudor monarchs. The initial break from the Papacy came over the matter of Henry VIII's divorce rather than any question of theology. When the young Edward VI succeeded Henry, his advisers advanced the cause of radical Protestantism. But when Edward died early, his half-sister Mary became Queen and promptly tried to restore Catholicism by force, burning Protestant martyrs at the stake. Her wiser successor Elizabeth set the Anglican Church on its characteristic middle course, neither Catholic nor Calvinist.

Probably the single most important religious development in Britain was the translation of the Bible commissioned by James I in 1604. This "Authorized" or "King James" version (which made use of previous translations) contains countless beautiful and memorable phrases that have entered, along with those of Shakespeare, into the English language and mind—at least until recently, when knowledge of either can no longer be presumed! The new technology of printing made the Bible available to anyone who could read, so people could now interpret the scriptures for themselves, unfiltered by church authority. We now take this for granted, so it is difficult for us to understand just how big a revolution it was.

In early 17th-century England, there was a sense of new opportunities, but also some uncertainty and insecurity. In the previous century England's power had expanded under the Tudors, especially after the defeat of the Spanish Armada in 1588. And now there began an emigration of English Puritans and radical Protestants to found new settlements in North America: the so-called "Pilgrim Fathers" and many more who were keen to escape religious repression. Intellectually, English literature had entered a golden age of poetry and drama, with its glorious peak in William Shakespeare's genius. Modern physical science was just getting going with the astronomical discoveries of Galileo, which disproved the old earth-centred cosmology that had been a fundamental part of the medieval Christian worldview. So there was a sense that human reason and practical ingenuity could change the world, but there was some worry about what such changes would mean.

There was a religious restiveness, a spiritual search for new or renewed forms of Christianity. The Elizabethan religious settlement did not please everybody, and many felt that the Anglican form of state-sponsored middle-of-the-road reformation remained woefully incomplete. Under the Stuart kings in the 17th century there developed a bitter power struggle between the Monarchy and Parliament. The conflict had a religious dimension, because Charles I tried to impose a "high" version of Anglicanism including bishops, vestments and ritual throughout the British Isles, even (ill-advisedly) on Presbyterian Scotland. The bulk of the English Parliamentary supporters were non-Anglican "Puritans", and they made a common anti-royalist cause with the Scots. In the 1640s it came to civil war, and when the Parliamentary armies eventually prevailed, Charles I was executed in 1649. In the 1650s Britain was briefly a republic, with Oliver Cromwell ruling as "Lord Protector", i.e. as King in all but name. But after his death, order broke down, and the monarchy and the Anglican Church were restored in 1660.

The Quaker movement started as one of the radically unorthodox religious sects that emerged in the ferment of religious, social and political ideas in the period of the Civil War and its uneasy aftermath. The war years provided an opportunity for new movements, when censorship lapsed and there was unprecedented intellectual and religious freedom. A confusing multitude of new groups grew up, including the Seekers, Ranters, Levellers, Separatists, Independents, Baptists, Anabaptists, Muggletonians, and Fifth Monarchists. The last had apocalyptic expectations of the imminent end of the world—and indeed, the national situation must have felt like the end of the world as people had known it. The Levellers wanted a society in which everybody would be equal, but they were firmly put down by Cromwell, whose "leveling" ambitions only went so far as the gentleman farming class from which he came. Apart from the Baptists, the Quakers are the only sect from that time to have survived down to the present day, due largely to the inspirational and organizing work of George Fox (1624–1691).

George Fox's Light of Christ Within

We get a vivid picture of Fox's life from the *Journal* that he dictated in middle age. It tells a breathless story in Joycean stream-of-consciousness style using 17th-century language that is sometimes strange and even coarse. We hear in great detail of his spiritual journey, beginning with his youthful "seeking", his many travels, beatings and imprisonments in the cause of spreading the Light as he saw it, and his eventual leadership of the Quaker movement and missionary journeys abroad, even to America. In contrast to the much more distant cases of Socrates and Jesus, there is plenty of evidence about Fox from his own writings, and from other Quakers.

George Fox was born into a humble family in the small village of Fenny Drayton (also known as Drayton-in-the-Clay) in South Leicestershire, at the geographical centre of rural pre-industrial England. Several Protestant martyrs had come from that district, and his mother was reputed to come from "martyr stock". Fox's father was a weaver and a churchwarden known as "Righteous Christer". Young George had little formal education. He was apprenticed to a local businessman, and he said that "a great deal went through my hands", which suggests he had early experience of agricultural business. This must have developed his practical shrewdness and ability to judge people's characters (people later remarked on his penetrating gaze).

Fox's *Journal* gives us only a brief summary of his early years. He comes over as an unusually serious youth, even rather "holier than thou". He relates an incident when he was on business at a fair, and was invited to drink a jug of beer with two other young men — nothing unusual in that, we might think! But what seems to have shocked young George was that his companions — who were "professors", people who had publicly professed their religious commitment — called for more beer, and proposed that whoever would not drink would pay for all. He was so pained by the contradiction between "profession" and action that he left the table, went home and prayed, and was unable to sleep that night. He reports that the Lord said to him: "Thou seest how young people go together into vanity, and old people into the earth; and thou must forsake all, both young and old, and keep out of all, and be a stranger unto all". No doubt it was more common in the 17th century than the 21st to believe that God had spoken to oneself individually, but it need not have involved a publicly audible voice speaking from heaven, it may only have meant that a powerful conviction came over him, which he interpreted as the will of God. (Contemporary Quakers say this can happen in Quaker meetings, including even meetings for business.) Throughout the rest of his *Journal* Fox reports many such divine guidances or visions, which he called "openings".

In 1643 the 19-year-old George Fox obeyed what he saw as a commandment from God, left his employment and his family, and embarked on several years of wandering around the midlands of England, seeking spiritual guidance from whatever sources he could find. His relations wanted to see him safely married off, but he replied that he was still only a lad, and must get wisdom. His search was not easily satisfied: one priest recommended tobacco and psalms, and later it was put to him that he should join the army (presumably the Parliamentary one), but he refused. We might now describe such a person as a teenage drop-out (apparently he had the long hair too!). It is mysterious how he could afford to live, and we have to presume that his family or his own savings provided enough money to pay for his food and lodging. The other remarkable thing is that these were precisely the years of the civil war, and though he must have been aware of what was going on, the *Journal* hardly mentions the national conflict, so intense was his concentration on his own spiritual search (pp. 6–9).

GEORGE FOX AND THE BEGINNING OF THE QUAKERS

These were years of physical and mental suffering for Fox. He mentions many different priests and "professors" from whom he sought guidance, but he was constantly disappointed. One of his earliest "openings" was that being educated at Oxford or Cambridge did not qualify men to be ministers of Christ—a subversive thought indeed, for that time! Fox felt he could join neither the Anglicans nor "the Dissenting people" (the Puritans), but had "to rely wholly upon the Lord Jesus Christ" (pp. 10–11). He seems to have almost given up attending churches, but when he did he tended to interrupt with his own comments and objections, for which he suffered a number of beatings. He would take his Bible into the orchards and fields to study, and it must have been in this time that he acquired the encyclopedic knowledge of the Scriptures that he later used to such effect. Here was the newly translated Bible put into the hands of a relatively uneducated man who interpreted it for himself in quite radical ways, as we shall see.

The most fundamental feature of the spirituality and theology towards which Fox was struggling was the claim to the possibility of direct revelation of God within each person. The Lord "did not dwell in temples made with hands", but "in people's hearts", "there was an anointing within man, to teach him", and "the Lord would teach his people himself" (p. 11). (Fox used the masculine pronoun to refer to all humanity, but he firmly rejected the suggestion that women have no souls, and the Quakers shocked convention by allowing women to minister in their meetings for worship.) But what was the relation between his claimed individual revelations and what he read in the Bible? It seems to have been a two-way street:

> And when I had openings, they answered one another, and answered the Scriptures: for I had great openings of the Scriptures. (*Journal*, 1646–7, p. 12)

However in Fox's radically challenging view, the Scriptures can give us only second-hand knowledge:

> The knowledge which the world hath, of what the prophets and apostles spake, is a fleshly knowledge; and the apostates from the life, in which the prophets and apostles were, have gotten their words, the Holy Scriptures, in a form, but not in their life, nor spirit, that gave them forth. (*Journal*, 1646–7, p. 13)

The implication is that the mere knowledge of Biblical text does not in itself give us any spiritual insight, and nor does the academic study of the linguistic and historical background, useful though that may be. We need more than the words on the page or in the liturgy, we have to appropriate their meaning for our own lives. And that is always a matter of interpretation, needing input not just from us, but from divine illumination, i.e. the operation of the Holy Spirit (pp. 31-34). As Fox put it, he knew such things "experimentally", i.e. from direct experience; and in that he discovered spiritual joy:

> My desires after the Lord grew stronger, and zeal in the pure knowledge of God, and of Christ alone, without the help of any man, book or writing. For though I read the Scriptures, that spake of Christ, and of God; yet I knew him not, but by revelation, as he, who hath the key, did open, and as the Father of life drew me to his Son by his Spirit. And then the Lord did gently lead me along, and did let me see his love, which was endless and eternal, and surpassed all the knowledge, that men have in the natural state, or can get by history, or books. (*Journal*, 1646-7, p. 14)

But this divine Light also showed up human "darkness, death, temptations, the unrighteous, the ungodly" (as in *John* 1:5), and Fox found that "the spiritual discerning came into me, by which I could discern my own thoughts, groans and sighs; and what it was, that did veil me, and what it was, that did open me". (p. 16). In Nottinghamshire, he says, the Lord showed him "that the nature of those things, which were hurtful without, were within in the hearts and minds of wicked men" (p. 20). (No doubt the lesson—derived from Jesus's teaching at *Mark* 7:21-23—still needs to be learnt, in Nottinghamshire and everywhere else.) Fox then writes:

> I cried to the Lord, saying, "Why should I be thus, seeing I was never addicted to any of these evils?" And the Lord answered, that it was needful, I should have a sense of all conditions: how else should I speak to all conditions? And in this I saw the infinite love of God. I saw also, that there was an ocean of darkness and death: but an infinite ocean of light and love, which flowed over the ocean of darkness: and in that also I saw the infinite love of God; and I had great openings. (*Journal*, 1646-7, p. 21)

Towards the end of these years of spiritual struggle, he reports, in eloquent Biblical language reminiscent of the Garden of Eden, a sense of spiritual ecstasy:

> Now was I come up in spirit through the flaming sword into the paradise of God. All things were new, and all the creation gave another smell unto me, than before, beyond what words can utter. I knew nothing, but pureness, and innocency, and righteousness, being renewed in the image of God by Christ Jesus; so that I say, I was come up to the state of Adam, which he was in, before he fell. (*Journal*, 1648, p. 27)

The beginning of the Quaker movement

Now that Fox had discovered his own spiritual bearings, the feeling grew that he had a message to impart to others. He believed that the divine light and the sense of salvation that he had experienced so vividly was available to everyone:

> Now the Lord God hath opened to me by his invisible power, how that every man was enlightened by the divine light of Christ; and I saw it shine through all: and that they, that believed in it, came out of condemnation, and came to the light of life, and became the children of it; but they that hated it, and did not believe in it, were condemned by it; though they made a profession of Christ. (*Journal*, 1648, p. 33)

He started to "convince" people, and to attract crowds as "a young man that had a discerning spirit" (p. 22). The first name for his followers was "Children of Light", but there was as yet no formal organization; they were just some amongst many evolving groups of spiritual seekers in that turbulent time. Other fellow-workers and preachers joined the incipient movement, such as Elizabeth Hooton, James Nayler, William Dewsbury, Richard Farnsworth, Francis Howgill, Margaret Fell, and John Stubbs. It was never a one-man cult as so many others have been, and some women played important roles.

For the rest of his life Fox was an itinerant preacher, traveling the length and breadth of England, Wales, and Scotland, with later visits to Ireland, Holland and America, interrupted only by several periods of imprisonment. He must have had a very robust physical constitution, for travel in those days was strenuous, on foot or horseback; he writes of hungry nights spent under hedges, and of severe beatings up; and prison conditions were often barbarous and filthy. His message emphasized individual religious experience, but he was also very practical about people's need for the support of a spiritual community, and he strongly encouraged his followers to establish local groups. These would meet regularly in private houses or outdoors, with no set liturgy or ritual or sacraments, nor pre-selected Bible readings; typically the meeting would wait in reverent, expectant silence until any of its members felt spontaneously moved "by the Spirit" to read, pray, preach, or otherwise share a spiritual insight.

Fox's religious ethics

Fox's message was not *purely* religious; he rejected any notion that the "religious" is a special dimension distinct from the rest of life (as may seem to be suggested by Jesus's saying: "Pay to Caesar what is Caesar's, and to God what is God's"). Fox reports that in 1648 "the Lord opened to him" that the three traditional professions were out of joint: the physicians (doctors) were "out of the wisdom of God" because they "knew not the virtues of the creatures" (i.e. they were ignorant of the true nature of living bodies); the priests "were out of the true faith, which Christ is the author of"; and the lawyers were "out of equity, and out of true justice, and out of the law of God" (p. 28). One can well imagine members of all these professions protesting that this arrogant young radical did not know what he was talking about! Yet he had a point, in each case. Medical knowledge was primitive by our standards, the circulation of the blood had only just been discovered by William Harvey and treatments like bloodletting were based only on tradition and folklore; Fox himself was credited with many remarkable healings of body and mind, which he himself attributed to the power of the Lord (p. 42). As for the divines, we have already seen how he thought the priests of the established church had been led away from the fundamental experience of Christianity by many centuries of tradition. And lawyers are always open to the temptation of exploiting their position in their own interests rather than those of their clients. At Mansfield, Fox felt it "upon him from the Lord" to speak to the justices not to oppress the servants in their wages—though he also exhorted the servants to do their duties and serve honestly (pp. 26–27). At Twycross, he was moved to warn the excise-men not to oppress the poor (pp. 45–46).

Fox and his followers were socially subversive in other ways. They refused to swear oaths, as was common practice in legal and political contexts. In this, they took Jesus's injunction at *Matthew* 5:34 quite literally, backing it up with the argument that swearing an oath to be truthful in court implies a double standard, suggesting that one feels free to be less scrupulous elsewhere. There were more everyday occasions of offence, too. Fox felt forbidden by the Lord to take off his hat to people of superior social status, and used "thee" and "thou" to them, when the practice of the time was to say 'you'. He would not "bow or scrape with his leg" to anyone, nor even say 'Good Morrow' or 'Good Evening'. The latter seems excessive to us, but his main point was to witness to the equality of every human being in the sight of God (Quakers call this the testimony to equality). In a strongly hierarchical society many people found the refusal to go in for the conventional pleasantries as extremely rude, and potentially seditious. For Fox however, this sort of honouring was "an honour invented by men in the Fall", "an honour which proud flesh looked for", "but Christ will have none of it" (p. 36). However, his particular judgments can be questioned: it is a delicate matter to decide how far one should go along with social conventions, and when to object on principle. (I have not heard of Quakers refusing to say *vous* and *Sie* when speaking to strangers in French and German!)

Fox had much to say about social ethics. In 1649 he reports that he was "sorely exercised" in exhorting the judges and justices to do justly, and in warning those who "kept public houses for entertainment, that they should not let people have more drink, than would do them good" (*plus ca change, plus c'est la meme chose!*). He also testified against wakes or feasts, May-games, sports, plays and shows, against deceitful merchandise, cheating and cozening, and against all sorts of music, and "mountebanks playing tricks on their stages; for they burdened the pure life, and stirred up people's minds to vanity". He exhorted schoolteachers and parents to train up their children in the fear of the Lord, and to be examples of sobriety and virtue themselves (p. 38). All this from a mere 25-year-old unmarried youth with no settled employment—it was enough to give Puritanism a bad name! Exhortation may have its occasional place, but the power of example tends to be greater, as Fox and the Quakers usually showed. I do not know what sort of music or plays so aroused his ire; probably it was low-level popular stuff rather than Tallis or Shakespeare. It is only in the last century or so that Quakers have relaxed this very austere line on the arts, but the question of the moral content and influence of the media and what passes as "the entertainment industry" is still very relevant. In 1651 Fox was moved to protest against the imposition of the death penalty for theft; he also wrote "what a sore thing it was that prisoners should lie so long in gaol: and how that they learned badness one of another in talking of their bad things" (p. 56) (*plus ca change* ...). In some other respects Fox did *not* challenge the beliefs of his time. He occasionally refers to witchcraft, and he says he was once accused of using it himself. On several occasions he publicly told a woman she was a witch, and he reports that all the country agreed with him (pp. 117, 120). He also seems to have taken talk of the Devil quite literally (pp. 322-3, 387, 436).

In the *Journal* for 1651 there is a rare reference to national events. Fox was imprisoned in a "House of Correction" in Derby at the time when the executed king's son (the future Charles II) had been trying to organize a fightback against the new national order, the "Commonwealth". A battle at Worcester was imminent, and the authorities were recruiting troops from the prison. Fox was offered the position of captain, but he refused it with eloquent but uncompromising, even truculent, words:

> I told them that I lived in the virtue of that life and power that took away the occasion of all wars: and I knew from whence all wars did rise from the lust according to James his doctrine: and they still courted me to accept of their offer: and thought I did but compliment with them but I told them that I was come into the covenant of peace which was before wars and strifes was: and they said they offered it in love and kindness to me because of my virtue and such like: and I told them if that was their love and kindness I trampled it under my feet. (*Journal*, 1651, p. 54)

Unsurprisingly, he was put back in prison, this time in a stinking dungeon alongside rogues and felons. Many Quakers have since followed his example of costly refusal of military service, especially during the First World War when they were severely punished.

With the excited growth of a new unorganized religious movement, there arose some strange behaviour by people who may have been associated with it. Some paraded in sackcloth and ashes, others took to going "naked", which seems to have meant wearing only underclothes, which was startling enough for the time! It is difficult to understand their motivation: they have been re-enacting what they read in the Old Testament, and perhaps like some modern demonstrations they were vividly expressing dissent from the established order of society. As we have seen, Fox himself felt no inhibition about interrupting church services and breaking social conventions. On one early occasion, he seems to have gone over the top. "Steeplehouse spires" sometimes set off his anger, and he reports that in 1651 seeing three of them "struck at his life", and when he was told that they belonged to the cathedral at Lichfield, he felt "commanded of the Lord" to hasten there over hedge and ditch, take off his shoes, and leave them with some astonished shepherds. Then, with "the word of the Lord like a fire in him" he entered the town and went up and down the streets crying "Woe unto the bloody city of Lichfield", until some "friendly people" came to him and said "Alack, George, where is thy shoes?" after which he retreated the way he had come (pp. 57-58). Afterwards he seems to have been puzzled by his own actions. He says that while he was shouting he had had a vision of blood running down the streets, and he was later given to understand that a thousand Christians had been martyred there in Roman times, so he tries to explain his puzzling "commandment" in terms of that. Perhaps his year of harsh imprisonment in Derby had somewhat unbalanced his mind. In the rest of his career he acted much more soberly.

Later on, Fox had to deal with some embarrassing tendencies in other Quakers. James Nayler was an enthusiastic young leader, but Fox began to worry about his judgment. He writes that "James Nayler run out and a company with him into imaginations" (p. 201). Nayler had felt led by an inner inspiration to ride into Bristol on the back of a donkey, with his young female followers hailing him like a messiah. The authorities took this as a claim to be the returning Christ, and Nayler was found guilty of blasphemy. In the brutal fashion of the time he was sentenced to 201 lashes, to branding on his forehead, and to have his tongue bored with a hot iron. This episode, a tabloid story of its time, threatened to bring the whole Quaker movement into disrepute. Fox publicly repudiated it, and was severe towards Nayler (p. 202). It became clear that there had to be some corporate discipline if the movement was to survive; any individual's claim to have seen the divine Light was fallible, and could be overridden by the judgment of the community.

Nayler survived his cruel punishments, and repented of his actions. In 1659 Fox still rebuffed his attempts at reconciliation, until William Dewsbury brought them together. Nayler died after a mugging in 1660, but left behind some immortal last words:

> There is a spirit, which I feel that delights to do no evil nor to revenge any wrong, but delights to endure all things, in hope to enjoy its own in the end. Its hope is to outlive all wrath and contention, and to weary out all exaltation and cruelty, or whatever is of a nature contrary to itself. ... In God alone it can rejoice, though none else regard it, or can own its life. ... I found it alone, being forsaken. I have fellowship therein with

those who live in dens and desolate places in the earth, who through death obtained this resurrection and eternal holy life. (QFP 19.12)

The growth of Quakerism

Relating the melodramatic Nayler episode has taken us a little ahead of our story. By this time the Quaker movement had made a breakthrough in the North-West of England. 1652 was the crucial year, when Fox travelled north into Yorkshire where many were convinced, and then crossed into Lancashire and was moved to climb to the top of Pendle Hill near Clitheroe, where, he says "the Lord let me see in what places he had a great people to be gathered". (This has entered into Quaker mythology, rather like Moses ascending the mountain in Sinai.) In this corner of 17th-century England, there was already much religious ferment, and many so-called Seekers, Separatists and Independents responded readily to Fox's message. A three-hour outdoor sermon from a rock on Firbank Fell on a June afternoon seems to have been one of the most effective of his whole ministry. Whole congregations joined the movement, and the northwest of England has been a stronghold of Quakerism ever since.

Fox moved on into Furness, an even more remote district of England separated from the south by the treacherous tidal sands of Morecombe Bay, and from the north by the Cumbrian mountains. There he made a connection that was to be crucial for him both personally and professionally. Just outside the small town of Ulverston lay Swarthmoor Hall, a 17th century manor house owned by Judge Thomas Fell, who had been a Member of Parliament in the crisis years of the 1640s. Fell and his wife Margaret were open and tolerant in outlook, and were already curious about the Quakers. When Fox arrived the Judge was away, but Margaret Fell and her daughters were soon convinced by Fox's message (pp. 90-91). A few weeks later he had a crucial interview with Judge Fell, who was so favorably impressed that he allowed the Quakers to meet in his house, though he did not actually join in (presumably because of his official position), but listened in from an adjoining room. Swarthmoor became the headquarters of the Quaker movement. Much later, after the Judge's death, George Fox and Margaret Fell were married in 1669. (The venerable Swarthmoor Hall still stands, and is now a Quaker conference centre.)

According to the *Journal* (p. 51) it was Justice Bennett of Derby in 1650 who first called Fox's followers "Quakers", because they bid him tremble at the word of God. In a variant tradition, it was because those who felt moved by the Spirit to put words into the silence of Meeting for Worship were wont to tremble (as can still happen). The name has stuck, and is a convenient abbreviation for the official title, which is now "The Religious Society of Friends" (they were first known as 'The Friends of Truth"). The abstract noun "Quakerism", although somewhat inelegant, has also entered into usage.

From 1653 onwards, the Quakers were becoming a movement of national importance, despite Fox enduring a spell in Carlisle Prison. They got into trouble for refusing to pay "tithes", the traditional taxes to support the established clergy. Also, the government could require anyone to swear an oath abjuring Catholicism, and since Quaker principles required the refusal of *all* oaths, this legislation could be deviously used against them. In 1655 Fox was arrested and brought before Oliver Cromwell, the supreme ruler of Britain at the time. Fox boldly "bid him keep in the fear of God that he might receive wisdom, that by it he might be ordered" (p. 151), and it is to Cromwell's credit that he did not take offence; indeed Fox reports that after many words with him, Cromwell said with tears in his eyes, "Come again to my house; for if thou and I were but an hour in a day together: we should be nearer one to the other" (p. 152). The 31-year-old preacher had acquired the power to impress the highest in the land. In 1656 he toured the South-West, and was imprisoned in Launceston in Cornwall, in the most disgusting and health-sapping conditions of all those he had to endure, in a pit of excrement known as "Doomsdale" (pp. 192-3). But by 1658 he was again ministering in the corridors of power, when he was asked to attend Cromwell's favourite daughter Lady Elizabeth Claypole on her deathbed. The opening words of his letter to her have become famous: "Be still and cool in thy own mind and spirit ... and then thou wilt feel the principle of God to turn thy mind to the Lord God". In 1659, with Cromwell dead and no stable government to replace him, plots and rumours were circulating, and Quakers were persecuted once more. Fox advised them "not to meddle with the powers of the earth".

In 1660 the monarchy was restored, albeit with reduced powers vis-a-vis Parliament. There was a vengeful spirit against the Commonwealth regime: they even dug up Cromwell's body and displayed his decaying head for the delectation of London's public. And there was a renewed determination that there should be only one form of religious worship in the realm. Charles II was himself inclined towards toleration, if only because he had no serious religious convictions apart from a certain taste for Catholicism (to which he converted on his deathbed). But the new Parliament of Royalist sympathizers and the re-established Anglican Church were determined to have their way with dissenters. After an incompetent attempt at a coup by the Fifth Monarchy Men in 1661, all religious dissent was stamped on. Although Fox drew up an eloquent public declaration that Quakers would never carry arms or violently opposed the government, this was of little avail. The Quaker Act and subsequent Conventicle Acts made it illegal to hold any non-Anglican religious service. Quakers refused to comply, and unlike other dissenters they did not attempt to hide their meetings. When adults were arrested, their children would carry on the meeting. This was the worst period of persecution for Quakers; thousands were imprisoned, and though none were actually executed, hundreds of them died in prison. (In the new Puritan theocracy of Masachushetts across the Atlantic, supposedly founded in the name of religious liberty, several Quakers were martyred.)

Later in his reign Charles II freed twelve hundred Quaker prisoners, and in 1682 his brother, the future James II, gave a patent for a new province in America to two prominent and well-connected Quakers, the theologian Robert Barclay (who we will meet in the next chapter) and the statesman William Penn who became the eponymous first leader of Pennsylvania. However the future of Britain was becoming unstable again. James, the heir to the throne, made no secret of his Catholicism, and again there were plots and rumours of plots. When James became King in 1685, he moved towards the re-Catholicizing of England, and to that end, he issued a Declaration of Indulgence in 1687 that suspended all penal laws affecting religion, thus allowing freedom of worship to all. Very admirable, we may think—but his motivation was to protect Catholics, and in unilaterally cancelling Parliament's legislation he threatened to re-ignite the civil war. The rich and powerful classes felt they could not have that all over again, and called in William of Orange, the ruler of the Netherlands and son-in-law of James II. William landed with his Dutch soldiers, James' army refused to fight, the King himself fled to France, and "the Glorious Revolution" of 1688 was over without a drop of blood. From then on Parliament—or whoever who could control it!—was firmly in power. The Toleration Act of 1689 allowed freedom of public worship to all who accepted the Bible and the Trinity, and rejected transubstantiation and the Pope. The

Quakers qualified — though whether they still accept the doctrine of the Trinity is a matter of subtle theology. In 1696 they were allowed to make a solemn promise instead of swearing an oath. From that time on they have been a respected minority sect, with unorthodox beliefs, and an ethical scrupulosity that many have found inconvenient.

Before closing this chapter, let us return to George Fox's own story. In the Restoration period he experienced again the top and the bottom of society: he was imprisoned at Lancaster, Scarborough, and Worcester, and he lobbied in London on behalf of the Quaker movement. The time of persecution required hard work to organize practical support and legal defence for those in prison; thus arose the "Meeting for Sufferings", a historical title still used for a central Quaker committee. Fox was also much involved in setting up a permanent organizational structure, by which a gentle kind of corporate discipline has held Quakers together at local and national level. No single individual or local group can go their own way: any claimed "illumination" or "concern" should be tested by a larger body. Meetings for business are seen as meetings for worship, in which the group as a whole tries to discern the will of God, without voting. In his later years, Fox made strenuous pastoral journeys to Ireland, the West Indies, the North American colonies, and Holland. He died in 1691, confident that the future of the movement was secure. Let us give the last word to Fox himself:

> ... the true light which enlightened every man that cometh into the world was the life in the word and that was divine and not natural ...
>
> And wicked men was enlightened by this light else how could they hate it. And the reason why they did hate it was because their deeds were evil and they would not come to it because it reproved them and that must needs be in them that reproved them.
>
> And that light could not be the Scriptures of the New Testament for it was before the four evangelists and the Epistles and Revelations was written. So it must be the divine light which is the life in Christ, the word before Scripture was written: and the grace of God which brought salvation had appeared unto all men: which taught the saints. (*Journal*, 1664 p. 341)

Further reading

Will Durant, *The Story of Civilization: Part VI: The Reformation* (New York: Simon and Schuster 1957)

In Oxford University Press's Very Short Introduction series, there are books on *The Reformation* by Peter Marshall, on *Martin Luther* by Scott H. Hendrix, and on *The Quakers* by Pink Dandelion.

Alister E. McGrath, *Christian Theology: An Introduction* (Oxford: Blackwell, 3rd edition 2001), Ch.3

Christopher Hill, *Intellectual Origins of the English Revolution Revisited* (Oxford University Press 1997) is a classic work by a master historian of the 17th century.

George Fox's *Journal* is available in several editions. My page references are to the Penguin Classics edition, edited by Nigel Smith (Penguin 1998). There is also an edition by John L. Nickalls (Cambridge University Press 1952, reprinted by London Yearly Meeting in 1975).

Truth of the Heart: an anthology of George Fox's writings, selected and annotated by Rex Ambler (London: Quaker Books 2001)

Joseph Pickvance, *George Fox on the Light of Christ Within* (New Foundation Publications no.3, George Fox Fund 1984) is a detailed short study of Fox's theology.

George Fox and the Quakers, by Cecil W. Sharman (Quaker Home Service, London, and Friends United Press, Richmond, Indiana, 1991) is a very readable and informative biography of Fox in the context of his times.

300 Years of Friends, by Howard Brinton (George Allen & Unwin, 1953) is an illuminating account of the original and continuing inspiration of Quakerism.

An Introduction to Quakerism, by Pink Dandelion (Cambridge University Press, 2007) is a sociological survey of Quaker history, including the many schisms in America and the varieties of Quakerism around the world today.

Quaker Faith and Practice: The book of Christian discipline of the Yearly Meeting of the Religious Society of Friends (Quakers) in Britain (fourth edition, with revisions approved, 1995, 2005, 2009)

CHAPTER 7
LIGHT OR ENLIGHTENMENT?

Inward light?

George Fox was not a theologian, and certainly not a philosopher: he was something more than either—a spiritually inspired person who was inspirational to many others. But we should not avoid the hard questions that arise about his claims to have discerned "the Light of Christ" in his "openings". The general conception of divine light was not new: it was to be found in Plato, the neo-Platonists, St. Augustine and many others (Fox was no scholar, and seems to have read little other than the Bible). Yet however attractive we may find this conception, we have to address the fundamental epistemological problem about such inner illuminations, inspirations, visions, or revelations—how do we know whether any of them are true?

Fox and the early Quakers obviously thought of themselves as Christians: there wasn't much alternative in 17th-century Britain. But they were Christians of an unusual and unorthodox kind, for they did without creeds, priests, and sacraments, relying instead on the "inner light of Christ", and the spontaneous movement of the Holy Spirit to inspire people to "minister" (i.e. pray or speak) in Quaker Meetings for Worship. They claimed to be reviving "primitive Christianity", before the churches got organized. William Penn expressed their claimed inspiration in 1694:

> The Light of Christ within, who is the Light of the world and so a light to you that tells you the truth of your condition, leads all that take heed unto it out of darkness into God's marvelous light, for light grows upon the obedient. (*Quaker Faith and Practice* 26.44)

The concept of the inner or "inward" Light has been fundamental to Quaker spirituality ever since. It is still there in the *Advices and Queries* (which is the nearest thing the Quakers have to a creed, though it is rather an expression of a whole way of life):

> Take heed, dear Friends, to the promptings of love and truth in your hearts. Trust them as the leadings of God whose Light shows us our darkness and brings us to new life. (*Advices and Queries* no 1 in *Quaker Faith and Practice*)

But there is a crucial problem here. How do we know *which* of our inner illuminations or leadings really come from God? (For those who do not go in for "God"-language, there is a parallel question as to which of our moral intuitions, putative insights, or gut feelings are valid.) How can we tell which are the promptings of love and truth, and which are prompted by selfishness, pride, vanity, ambition, resentment, jealousy, nationalism, sexism, racism, etc.? How can we know when we are seeing things in "the Light of God", and when we are only seeing them in the light of fallible, and perhaps corrupt, human considerations? This is not just an academic question, it is a vital practical problem that we all have to face up to in our spiritual lives.

Robert Barclay's "immediate revelations" and Descartes' "natural light"

In Fox's own lifetime a second-generation Quaker offered a perhaps over-confident response to the question. Robert Barclay was an able young Scottish theologian who set out a Quaker theology in 15 propositions, explained and defended in some 400 pages. Such an exercise is rather out of keeping with the general suspicion by Quakers of intellectual theorizing, but if one has the patience to explore its 17th-century wordiness, one can find much that is in the spirit of Quakerism. The full-length title runs as follows:

> An Apology for the True Christian Divinity, as the same is held forth and preached by the people, in scorn, called Quakers; being a full explanation and vindication of their Principles and Doctrines, by many arguments deduced from scriptures and right reason, and the testimonies of famous authors, both ancient and modern, with a full answer to the strongest objections usually made against them.

Mercifully it is known for short as Barclay's *Apology*, first written in Latin, and published in English in 1678, with a respectful but by no means fawning prologue addressed to Charles II.

A question that arises for Quaker theology is whether there is any distinction between the Light and the Holy Spirit. Fox sometimes talked of "that Light and Spirit" in the same breath, as if these were two alternative words for the same thing, and he also talked of "the Word", following the prologue of John's gospel. The capital letters express the belief that the Light or Spirit or Word comes from God, and hence has authority and conveys nothing but truth. So what is meant is not just any old thought or image, prompting or impulse that comes to mind, but only those that strike home as true, revelatory, and putatively of divine authority. Fox emphasized that the light he was talking about is the *divine* Light, not natural, and that it can be described as the Light of *Christ*. It is sometimes called the "inner", sometimes the *"inward"*, light — and the latter word more accurately expresses the claim to its origin from outside the mind, and hence its objectivity, truth or validity. As we saw in the previous chapter, Fox even claimed that it pre-existed the Scriptures, for he says it was needed for writing them, and is still needed for their correct interpretation. There is a trace of Trinitarian theology in his thought here, for he implies that the Light is co-eternal with God the Father and God the Son, and it seems that "the inward Light" is an alternative name for the inspiration of the Holy Spirit. Barclay treats it as such, so his theology of immediate revelations can also be described as a theology of the Holy Spirit. (Perhaps this can do something to rescue this third member of the Trinity from its "Cinderella" status that we noted in Chapter 5.)

Barclay's most crucial proposition is his second, "Concerning Immediate Revelation", and I need to quote from his formulation at some length:

> ... the testimony of the Spirit is that alone by which the true knowledge of God hath been, is, and can be only revealed ...
>
> ... these divine inward revelations, which we make absolutely necessary for the building up of true faith, neither do nor can ever contradict the outward testimony of the scriptures, or right and sound reason. Yet from hence it will not follow, that these divine revelations are to be subjected to the examination, either of the outward testimony of the scriptures, or of the natural reason of man, as to a more noble or certain rule and touchstone; for this divine revelation, and inward illumination, is that which is evidence and clear of itself, forcing, by its own evidence and clearness, the well-disposed understanding to assent, irresistibly moving the same thereunto; even as the common principles of natural truths move and incline the mind to a natural assent; as, that the whole

is greater than its part; that two contradictory sayings can neither be both true, nor both false ...

Barclay is claiming that these divine inward illuminations can never contradict scripture or reason, and moreover that they do not need to be tested by appeal to scripture or reason. His comparison with the "irresistible" force of "natural truths" such as mathematical axioms suggests that he knew about Descartes' appeal to such self-evident truths, and wanted to claim the same kind of unassailable certainty for Quakerly inner illuminations.

But a similar epistemological problem arose at the foundations of Descartes' philosophy. In that same decade of the 1640s when the uneducated George Fox was setting out on his spiritual quest in the English midlands, Réné Descartes, France's greatest philosopher and scientific pioneer of the time, was thinking deeply about the foundations of philosophy, science, and religion. (There is no evidence that either knew anything about the other.) Descartes did not claim divine inspiration (except perhaps in a famous dream he had when beginning his philosophical project), and in his writings he appeals only to human reason. Yet he hoped that his conclusions would be acceptable to the Roman Catholic Church, and he was careful (after Galileo's renunciation of sun-centred astronomy, enforced by threats of torture at the hands of the Inquisition) to leave all religious matters to the authority of the Church.

Descartes' set of six *Meditations* is one of those masterpieces of intellectual provocation to which philosophers keep returning with fascination. In literary form they are in the genre of spiritual exercises in which the reader is invited to follow a course of soul-searching and self-improvement; but in Descartes' case the programme is rigorously intellectual rather than spiritual. In the first Meditation he raises radically sceptical doubts, and ends up wondering whether anything exists outside his own mind. However his intention was to *defeat* scepticism by putting all our beliefs through the test of his "method of doubt", to find which are really certain, so that knowledge can be rebuilt on a firm foundation. The point of his famous statement "I think, therefore I am" was that he could not doubt that he was thinking (because to doubt is, after all, one kind of thinking), therefore he could be certain that he himself existed, at least as a thinking mind. Moreover, he found various ideas and thoughts in his own mind, and he argued (very controversially) that these provide a basis for proving the existence of an omnipotent and benevolent God. He thought that this gives us a guarantee that our faculties will not deceive us if we use them carefully, so that our scientific inquiries can proceed with confidence.

But, in offering his purely rational proofs of the existence of God Descartes appealed to premises that he claims are given "by the natural light", but which most of his readers have *not* found at all obvious (namely the principles that there must be at least as much reality in a cause as in its effect, and that existence itself counts as a "perfection" or property). So the question arises whether "clear and distinct perception" or "seeing by the natural light" is really a guarantee of truth. Descartes does not address the question of how to resolve any differences of opinion that arise over what is "given by the natural light", the light of reason. And this failure vitiates his whole system, for it means that he cannot take for granted some of the crucial premises that he helps himself to.

The moral of this philosophical story is that there is no hope of building all our knowledge on foundations that are infallibly certain. Of course whatever is necessarily true cannot be false, but it does not follow that whatever someone thinks or "intuits", or seems "clearly and distinctly to perceive" to be a necessary truth, is *indeed* necessarily true. Our judgment of necessary truth is fallible, as anyone who has made mistakes in arithmetic or logic has ruefully to admit. Some philosophers have followed Descartes' assumption that if anything is to be so much as probable, something must be certain; but others (to my mind, more wisely) have embraced a thoroughly fallibilist epistemology. The 20th-century philosopher of science Karl Popper replaced the image of building our empirical and scientific knowledge on bedrock by that of founding it on a large number of piles driven into a swamp, with the implication that any one them can be shaken or replaced without destabilizing the whole structure.

There is a parallel point in religious epistemology about putative divine illuminations. Whatever is communicated by God must be true—that is a necessary truth given the standard conception of God: it is a rule of the language-game of "God"-talk (and even those who do not play the game can understand that it is a rule of the game). But it does not follow that whatever someone (whether Jane Bloggs offering "ministry" in a Quaker meeting one Sunday morning, or George Fox himself feeling inspired to proclaim woe to the city of Lichfield) *takes* to be given by divine illumination, the Light of Christ, or the inspiration of the Holy Spirit, really has that status. Our apprehension of religious truth (if there is such a thing at all) is always fallible.

I suggest, therefore, that we should reject Barclay's suggestion that putative divine revelations are not to be tested by appeal to the scriptures, or to the natural reason of man. Given our disagreements and our fallibility even about the most important matters, and the weird and wonderful (and sometimes terrible) things that various cult leaders have claimed to be the message of God, there is often a need to undertake further testing of putative divine illuminations. To his credit, Barclay later acknowledges the distinction I am insisting on:

> For it is one thing to affirm, that the true and undoubted revelation of God's Spirit is certain and infallible; and another thing to affirm, that this or that particular person or people is infallibly led by this revelation in what they speak or write, because they affirm themselves to be so led by the inward and immediate revelation of the Spirit. The first is only asserted by us, the later may be called in question. (*Apology*, II.xiii)

But unfortunately he does not adhere to this insight in his opening summary quoted above, or when he says at the end of the section that if asked "How dost thou know that thou art actuated by the Spirit of God?" we can dismiss the question as just as ridiculous as the question how one knows that the sun is shining at noonday, when one is there outdoors with one's eyes open. For our senses are subject to illusions and dreams and drugs, so not even the judgment that one can now see the sun shining is literally infallible. Barclay gives the unfortunate impression that he is offering a Quaker theology of infallible inner illumination by the divine Light or Holy Spirit, to contrast with Protestant belief in the infallibility of scripture, or Roman Catholic doctrine of the infallibility of the Pope or Church. I suggest that what we need to conclude is that there is no infallible means of recognition of religious truth, and that we need to compare and contrast traditions and scriptures, reason and scientific evidence, and the experience of many people, and remain "open to new light, from whatever source it may come" (*Quaker Advices and Queries* no. 7).

The Quakers in Britain have been a fairly small sect, subject to occasional changes of direction and emphasis. After the inspirations and persecutions of the 17th century, they had a quietist period in the following century when they became "a peculiar people" distinguishing themselves from the rest of society by dress and manners, and disapproving of "marrying out". They went through a somewhat evangelical phase in the 19th century, but since the Manchester conference of 1895 British Quakerism has become extremely "liberal" in its theology, to the point where in recent years many Quakers hesitate or equivocate about whether they even believe in God. (I will try to address that fundamental issue in Chapter 9.) However there are Quaker traditions in Africa and America who are rather more like evangelical Christians in their theology and practice, though they tend to retain some element of silent worship.

Fallibilism in identifying the Light or Spirit

A sharp distinction between divine and natural lights was made in 1879 by the Quaker Yearly Meeting in London:

> The light that shines into man's heart is not of man, and must ever be distinguished both from the conscience which it enlightens and from the natural faculty of reason which, when unsubjected to its holy influences, is, in the things of God, very foolishness. ... (*Quaker Faith and Practice* 26.63)

L. Hugh Doncaster, writing in 1972, provides a very helpful exploration of the way in which any individual experience of "light" should be tested and checked against the experience and affirmations of other people down the ages:

> This central affirmation, that the Light of the Christ-like God shines in every person, implies that our knowledge of God is both subjective and objective. It is easy to misconstrue "Inner Light" as an invitation to individualism and anarchy if one concentrates on the subjective experience known to each one. But it is an equally important part of our faith and practice to recognize that we are not affirming the existence and priority of your light and my light, but of the Light of God, and of the God who is made known to us supremely in Jesus. The inward experience must be checked by accordance with the mind of Christ, the fruits of the Spirit, the character of that willed caring which in the New Testament is called Love. It is further checked by the fact that if God is known in measure by every person, our knowledge of him will be largely gained through the experience of others who reverently and humbly seek him. In the last resort we must be guided by our own conscientiously held conviction—but it is in the last resort. First we must seek carefully and prayerfully through the insights of others, both in the past and among our contemporaries, and only in the light of this search do we come to our affirmation. (*Quaker Faith and Practice* 26.65)

Note here the distinction between "light" with a small "l" and with a capital. The capitalization indicates an objective truth—"the Light of God"; the small letter stands for an individual's subjective, fallible claim—"my light" is my present judgment about what the true Light of God is.

I find confirmation of this from a perhaps unexpected source in a sermon by Austin Farrer, an Oxford Anglo-Catholic theologian who has been described as the one genius of Anglicanism in the 20th century. In a sermon entitled "Inspiration by the Spirit" he mentioned two cases in which, he says, people identified mistaken human judgments as the inspiration of the Holy Spirit. One was a lady who had refused her doctor's recommendation to have her leg amputated, because she claimed that the Holy Ghost had said to her "Miss Barker, don't you have it off". The result was that she was bedridden for the rest of her life, useless to herself and a burden to others. Farrer concludes that it was not the Holy Spirit speaking within Miss Barker, it was only her animal fear of the surgeon's knife. This was a case of the heart going mistakenly against the head.

The second example was of a young woman who joined an enthusiastic religious group, and promptly fell in love with another recent convert, a man of formerly bad life. They planned to marry, but then she felt last minute doubts about whether he really loved her. She shared her doubts with the religious group; they laid the matter before the Lord in prayer, and the leader declared that the guidance of the Spirit was that the marriage should go forward. In the event, the man relapsed into his former ways, left the Christian group and abandoned his wife and their children. This was a case of the head (here, the prayerful judgment of the group leader) going mistakenly against the heart (the woman's intuition that the relationship was not strong enough to build a marriage on). Farrer drew a general lesson from these examples:

> The trouble about an indiscreet belief in inspiration is that it smothers reason. A man who declares "This is what the Spirit directs" is not required to give a reason; surely God does not argue his cases. But I say to you, always suspect claims to inspired guidance which bypass reasoned argument. There are not fewer reasons for what God ordains than for other things; there are more, far more. There are all the reasons in the world, if we can but find them. For is not he wise? (*The End of Man*, p. 64)

But does inspiration by the Spirit, or seeing something in the Light, then come down merely to using our own human judgment as best we can? We seem to face the following dilemma: either your supposed leadings by the Spirit or Light come without reasons (and perhaps even run contrary to reason) — in which case they are irrational, and should not be trusted, or else there are what we can recognize as good reasons for them — in which case it is precisely those reasons that justify following them, and appeal to the Spirit or the Light is superfluous. Farrer recognized this dilemma, and offered a response to it. The Christian, he says, is inspired by the Spirit of Christ. And how does the Spirit of Christ shape our spirits? — by our developing (however imperfectly) the Christlike virtues of faith, hope, and love:

> These attitudes, so far as we Christians share them, are simply Christlike, simply divine, and no inspiration we could possibly receive could be higher or diviner than this. There is nothing better, in this life, that God could give us.
> ... The mind governed by Christ's faith, Christ's hope, Christ's love, is the mind that sees straight ...
> Between getting one's spiritual eyes, and claiming oracular inspirations, the difference is wide. Oracular assurances are a *substitute* for intellectual sight, whereas what we are talking about is a clearing of intellectual sight. (*The End of Man*, pp. 64–5)

Farrer ended that sermon with a very Quakerly invitation to deepen our entry into "the divine-human life of Christ" in the silence of a retreat, with its concentration on God, and the mutual support of the participants in seeking Him.

Locke on "enthusiasm" and "reason"

In the same generation as Robert Barclay, the English philosopher John Locke attacked "enthusiasm" in Book IV, Chapter xix of his famous *Essay concerning Human Understanding* (1690). The etymology of this word involves the conception of "a god within", and Locke obviously had in mind the disputes between rival religious sects that had caused such trouble in 17th century Britain. What he says about "illumination" makes it apparent that he would include the Quakers amongst the dangerous "enthusiasts", though he does not mention them by name:

> Whatever groundless opinion comes to settle strongly upon their fancies is an illumination from the Spirit of God, and presently of divine authority; and whatsoever odd action they find in themselves a strong

> inclination to do, that impulse is immediately concluded to be a call or direction from heaven and must be obeyed …
>
> Reason is lost upon them, they are above it; they see the light infused into their understandings, and cannot be mistaken: it is clear and visible there, like the light of bright sunshine, shows itself, and needs no other proof but its own evidence …
>
> This is the way of talking of these men: they are sure because they are sure, and their persuasions are right only because they are strong in them. (*Essay* IV.xix.6,8,9)

Thus Locke identifies his target. Then comes the nub of his philosophical criticism:

> But to examine a little soberly this internal light, and this feeling on which they build so much. … let me ask: This seeing, is it the perception of the truth of the proposition, or of this, that it is a revelation from God? …
>
> The question then here is: How do I know that God is the revealer of this to me, that this impression is made upon my mind by his Holy Spirit, and that therefore I ought to obey it? If I know not this, how great soever the assurance is that I am possessed with, it is groundless: whatever light I pretend to, it is but *enthusiasm*. (*Essay* IV.xix.10)

Locke warmly endorses our conclusion argued above, that any putative divine inner illumination should be tested by whatever else we take to be reliable sources of knowledge:

> He, therefore, that will not give himself up to all the extravagancies of delusion and error must bring this guide of his *light within* to the trial. God when he makes the prophet does not unmake the man. He leaves all his faculties in their natural state, to enable him to judge of his inspirations, whether they be of divine original or no. When he illuminates the mind with supernatural light, he does not extinguish that which is natural. (*Essay* IV.xix.14)

Locke goes on to declare that "Reason must be our last judge and guide in *everything*" (my italics)—a sentence which sounds like a clarion call to the "Age of Enlightenment" characteristic of the next century in Europe, the 18th. However Locke himself was a transitional figure in the history of thought. He still maintained that the existence of God could be proved by reason alone (*Essay* IV.x)—a claim which was to come under stringent philosophical criticism by Hume and Kant. The very bold-sounding assertion just quoted has to be understood in the context of Locke's acceptance that God has revealed Himself through Scripture, and above all in the story of Christ. What then is the relation between reason and revelation? Whatever God reveals must be true (assuming that God is as good as He is cracked up to be — which is, of course, a rule of this language-game!); but Locke insists that we have to use our natural powers of reason to recognize and understand God's speech, to *identify what counts* as divine revelation. In his view, the divinely-authorized status of Moses and Jesus was evidenced by miracles: God identified himself to Moses by "outward signs" such as the burning bush and the parting of the Red Sea, and the reports of Jesus's miracles are similarly supposed to attest to his divine status. According to Locke faith is the assent to a proposition not because of evidence directly in favour of it, rather "upon the credit of the proposer as coming from God, in some extraordinary way of communication", i.e. revelation (IV.xviii.2). Faith "can never convince us of anything that *contradicts* our knowledge", though "revelation, where God has been pleased to give it, must carry it against the *probable* conjectures of reason" (IV.xviii.5,8). Yet "it still belongs to reason to judge of the truth of its being a revelation and of the signification of the words wherein it is delivered" (IV.x.8,10). Given the crucial role that he ascribes to reason in religion, we can see why Locke entitled one of his later works *The Reasonableness of Christianity* (1695).

Locke's religious epistemology was unstable, however. Such efforts to make Christianity reasonable were (and still are) vulnerable to attack on two fronts: from the rationalists who do not find them reasonable, and from the fundamentalists who do not find them Christian. In particular, Locke's appeal to miracles was wide open to the sort of scepticism that was argued so forcefully by Hume in the next generation. Why should we believe reports of dramatic exceptions to the laws of nature, when all our other evidence of the workings of the world tells against them? And do we *need* any such fragile, disputable buttressing in order to be assured of the validity of the Mosaic Commandments, or the teaching of Jesus, or Confucius, or the Buddha? Surely their validity can "strike home", as it has done to many generations, quite independently of whatever we make of miraculous reports?

The Enlightenment

From the mid-17th century onwards, science became widely recognized as the only way to gain knowledge of the material world. Newton's theory of mechanics was triumphantly successful in explaining the motion of everything in the heavens and on the earth. The next big step was to apply scientific method to human beings. In the great European movement of ideas called the "Enlightenment", centered in the 18th century, there emerged a belief (or faith!) in the power of human reason to improve the human condition. It was thought that scientific rationality, applied to the critique of metaphysics and religion, to the benefit of individuals in medicine and education, and to the reform of human society in economics and politics, could lead to hitherto undreamed-of progress. In its more extreme versions, especially in some of the more radical French philosophers, this became the claim that science can replace *all* other guides to life, such as religion, morality, and the authority of monarchs and traditional governing classes. But not all Enlightenment philosophers were hostile to religion: as we have noted, Locke held on (if rather shakily) to Christianity, and as we will see in the next chapter, Kant offered a radically reinterpreted version of it.

In the 18th century 'enthusiasm' became a word of abuse for many thinkers in this "the Age of Reason". Religious enthusiasm — the claim of individuals to have discerned, or to have been vouchsafed, the light of God shining within their souls — was seen as subjective, capricious, and dangerous to the peace of the realm. After the Civil War and Glorious Revolution in Britain, and the more terrible wars of religion on the continent of Europe, it was attractive to replace such alleged individual illuminations by the light of reason, supposed to be equally discernable by anyone. There developed a separation of religion from politics, to which Locke made an influential contribution in his *Letter concerning Toleration* (1689), arguing eloquently for freedom of conscience and worship in religion, and for a clear distinction between church and state. (Quakers and other Protestant sects enjoyed liberty in Britain thereafter, though for at least another century there remained barriers to non-Anglicans entering the professions.)

In his *Second Treatise on Civil Government* (1690), Locke set out a doctrine of the natural rights of every person to life and liberty. This liberal philosophy has influenced the whole subsequent development of Western political thought, notably in the constitution of the newly-founded United States of America in the 1770s, with its declaration of the rights to life, liberty and "the pursuit of happiness", and its firm separation of religion and state. It is rather ironic that in Britain the separation is still incomplete, with the monarch remaining as head of the established Anglican Church and Anglican bishops sitting in the House of Lords, despite the fact that Britain has become, for better or for worse, a more secular society than the USA. Church attendance remains much higher in America, and Christianity (especially in Protestant evangelical form) has much more influence on American society, culture and politics, notoriously in resistance to Darwin's theory of evolution because it contradicts a literal reading of *Genesis*. Although the founding fathers of the USA were inspired by the secular ideals of the Enlightenment, there remains a deeply-entrenched influence of pre-Enlightenment Protestantism that was imported with the early Puritan settlers from northern Europe. Hence the continuing American "culture wars" between these two strands of their historical inheritance—political liberalism and religious conservatism.

It is also worth noting here that Islam, and to some extent Judaism and Eastern Orthodoxy, have not been through the same historical process as Western Christianity, namely Reformation leading to splits and wars of religion, followed by a gradual (often grudging) acceptance of a separation between religion and state, with religion being largely left—for better or for worse—as a matter for private conscience. Islam in one form or another has a dominating presence in many countries—notably Saudi Arabia, North Africa, Iran, Iraq, Pakistan, Afghanistan, and Indonesia, though the history and culture of these regions varies. But I think it is true to say that none of them has been through anything like the European Reformation and Enlightenment. (So much the better, some Muslim voices may say!) Certainly, the present cultural and religious and political differences between Islam and the West have deep historical roots—hence the problems in mutual understanding. As for Judaism, its history is different again, with nearly two millennia of Jewish minorities being scattered through many countries, and all too often persecuted. There was not a Jewish state between the years 70 and 1948. What to say about the relation between religion and politics in the new state of Israel, I leave to the reader to judge.

The Enlightenment took rather different forms in the rival nations of Western Europe. In Britain, which had been through the searing experience of civil war, there was a gradual evolution of politics and society. Democracy was introduced in fits and starts in a series of Reform Bills, and the vote was extended to women in the 1920s (the reform of the House of Lords is still not complete). In 18th-century France, still ruled by an absolute monarchy supported by a powerful aristocracy and the Catholic Church, the *philosophes* argued passionately for rational reform; but when the break finally came with the Revolution of 1789 it took a violently disruptive form. In Germany, still divided into a patchwork of small princely states, Enlightenment thought came late and was at first derivative from Britain and France, but it reached its fullest flowering in the thought of the towering figure of Kant, by most estimates the greatest philosopher since Plato and Aristotle, and the main figure in our next chapter.

Further reading

Barclay's Apology in Modern English, edited by Dean Freiday (Barclay Press 1991)

Quaker Faith and Practice: The book of Christian discipline of the Yearly Meeting of the Religious Society of Friends (Quakers) in Britain, in the edition published by them in 1995.

Austin Farrer, *The End of Man* (SPCK 1973).

In Oxford University Press's Very Short Introduction series, there are books on *Descartes* by Tom Sorell, and on *Locke* by John Dunn.

CHAPTER 8

KANT'S PHILOSOPHY OF RELIGION COMPARED TO QUAKERISM

I propose in this chapter to compare two things that have never to my knowledge been brought into connection, but both of which I have found appealing (there's no accounting for taste!) namely the heavyweight philosophy of Immanuel Kant and the unintellectual approach of the Quakers. I will suggest that on matters of religion they are surprisingly close.

Some Christian writers now express open hostility to the Enlightenment, assuming that such appeal to human reason is intrinsically inimical to true religion. (In Chapter 5 we found similar reactions in some Christian, Muslim and Jewish thinkers in the medieval period.) It is true that most of the French *philosophes* were hostile to Christianity, as was David Hume, the most radical philosopher of the Scottish Enlightenment (though not his distinguished successor Thomas Reid). But no one is entitled to make sweeping claims about the Enlightenment without making some effort to come to terms with the philosophy of Kant, who had some considerable sympathy for the claims of Christianity, though not perhaps in the orthodox interpretation of them — as I hope to explain.

Kant's philosophy

Kant spent his whole life (1724–1804) in the small Prussian city of Konigsberg, which was then on the eastern margin of European culture; but as a university professor in that centre of trade he was well-informed about the momentous intellectual, political and religious developments of the age.

Kant is typical of much modern Western thought in inheriting the twin influences of Christianity and science, and in struggling to combine the two.

His Christian inheritance included the conventional conceptions of God as omniscient, omnipotent and benevolent, and of an immortal human soul endowed with freewill and a sense of moral duty. But a more specific influence came from the Pietism of his parents. Pietism was a radical spiritual movement, a "religion of the heart" that had grown up within German Lutheranism, emphasizing personal devotion and right living above dogmas, creeds, and ritual—rather like the Quakers or Methodists in Britain. But by Kant's time Pietism had hardened into an insistence on stereotyped confessions of individual conversion, which Kant as a schoolboy found oppressive. However the pietist spirit is apparent in his later emphasis on good character and conduct as the only essential thing in religion.

Kant always saw his thought as contributing, however indirectly, to human progress. He resolutely defended the free use of reason to examine everything however traditional, authoritative or sacred, which made him a standard-bearer of the German Enlightenment. The word 'critique' (in the title of his three main works) meant for Kant the self-conscious philosophical inquiry into the powers and limitations of the human mind. He thus made epistemology (the study of what we can and cannot know) the heart of philosophy. Yet he also had a deep respect for ordinary moral feeling, and towards the end of his *Critique of Pure Reason* (1781), which contains some of the most abstruse philosophizing ever, he wrote:

> In regard to the essential ends of human nature even the highest philosophy cannot advance further than the guidance that nature has also conferred on the most common understanding. (A831/B859)

In his old age when his international reputation was assured, Kant got into trouble with his government. For most of his life he had benefited from the comparatively liberal rule of Frederick the Great of Prussia, but after that monarch's death a more reactionary regime took over. Its censors detected an unorthodox tendency in Kant's late writings on religion, and forbade him to publish any more on the subject. There was no question of execution like Socrates or the medieval heretics, but once again it was the alleged subversion of official religion that got a philosopher into conflict with power. Kant's response was wily: he gave a promise to obey, but worded it so that he felt bound only for the lifetime of Frederick William II, whom he managed to outlive.

In his epoch-making *Critique of Pure Reason* Kant explored the limits of knowledge, and diagnosed how we keep trying to go beyond them. We can only know things "as they appear", i.e. as they are perceived and conceptualized through the basic structures of our minds. Yet we still yearn for impossible metaphysical knowledge of things "as they are in themselves" — especially about our souls, the universe as a whole, and God. Such claims have long been central to theology, but according to Kant they are beyond our knowledge. His view is that although we can *understand* such assertions (they are not meaningless), we can neither prove nor disprove them, nor can we find probable scientific evidence for them. This makes a decisive break with the project of natural theology, namely the effort to provide rational proofs or scientific evidence for the existence of God (though many intelligent people still try to do it!). But there has long been a fideist vein in religion, exemplified in such different thinkers as Augustine, al-Ghazalli, Pascal and Kierkegaard, which holds that faith goes beyond reason (without being contrary to reason). When Kant famously wrote that he "denied knowledge to make room for faith" (he was denying knowledge of things as they are in themselves), he seems to be aligning himself with that tradition. Whether that is the whole story, we shall see.

In his moral philosophy Kant strongly emphasized the distinction between our self-interest and our moral duties, and he sternly insists that actions are good only if motivated by the latter. He contrasts our human nature with the animals on one side and with the conception of a "holy will" on the other. Animals feel no tension between desires and duty, for they do not have the concept of duty. A rational being without self-interested desires (such as an angel?) would also not experience any such tension, but for the opposite reason: not being subject to temptation, they would always do the right thing. Human beings are mixed creatures, midway between animals and angels. We are finite beings with our individual needs, and these include not just physical desires, but emotional needs and drives for love, approval, status and power; yet we are also rational beings, aware of moral obligations. We can never achieve perfection, and that tension is an inescapable feature of the human condition.

Kant's notion of moral freedom or autonomy is sometimes misunderstood as implying that we each have to decide our own values, as 20th century existentialists like Sartre said. But Kant was very definite about the absoluteness and objectivity of moral duties (indeed more so than most of us are prepared to be, for he held that one should *always* tell the truth and keep one's promises, even if the consequences are dreadful, and that one may *never* commit suicide). Moral claims are for Kant just as objective as those of mathematics and science, but they have a different *kind* of truth. I suggest that one main point behind his talk of autonomy is that as mature adults we should be able to make moral judgments without having to depend on someone else's authority, just as in teaching arithmetic we hope that our pupils will learn to do it for themselves. And if Christians (or Jews, or Muslims) rush in to condemn Kantian autonomy as an expression of sinful pride, I would refer to them to the passage where he talks of the moral law "humiliating" every human being.

It was Kant's last major work, *Religion within the boundaries of mere reason* (1793) that got him into trouble with the Prussian censorship. Its very title implies a challenge, for as we have seen, rational accounts of religion usually come under fire from traditionalist believers. Kant's hope was to distinguish the essential (and supposedly *reasonable*!) core of all religion from the inessential, optional extras that the various world religions add on. In it he displays considerable sympathy for the Christian tradition, but he proposes to interpret its claims symbolically rather than literally (like some other thinkers we have considered). His approach is summed up in a passage from his lecture-course on anthropology:

> In exhibiting concepts (called ideas) that belong to morality and therefore to pure reason, concepts which constitute the essence of all religion, it is *enlightenment* to distinguish the symbolic from the intellectual (public worship from religion), the temporarily useful and necessary *shell* from the thing itself. (*Anthropology from a Pragmatic Point of View*, 7:192)

Does the Religious Society of Friends exemplify Kant's ethical community?

Let me start with the externals, namely churches and religious groups as social institutions. Kant addressed these issues in Parts Three and Four of the *Religion*. (My references to this work will use the standard numbering-system that is used in all recent editions and translations.) As we will see Kant was fairly minimalist about the content of "pure religious faith", yet he saw a need for institutional religion to help transform human society in the right direction. Indeed, he held that human beings have a duty to join an "ethical community" under laws of virtue, seen as divine commands (6:94–9). But Kant's concept of an ethical community is an ideal to which particular churches or religious communities only imperfectly approximate. For him, a "true (visible) church is one that displays the (moral) kingdom of God on earth inasmuch as the latter can be realized through human beings". Such a church would be founded on universal moral principles; it should be "cleansed of the nonsense of superstition and the madness of enthusiasm"; its constitution should be neither monarchical (under a pope or patriarch), nor aristocratic (under bishops or prelates), nor democratic (ruled by those who claim to be directly illumined by God), rather it will be more like a household or family under a common though invisible moral father (6: 100-2). It has been suggested that a better model for this is the relationship of *friendship*, extended to encompass anyone.

The constitution and practice of the Religious Society of Friends seem pretty close to Kant's requirements. There is no appeal to authoritative revelation or miracles, no rituals except the practice of meeting for an hour of silent worship, and no sacraments (there are procedures for admission into membership, and for weddings and funerals). There are no professional priests or pastors, and it is open to anyone present to speak spontaneously (to "minister") in the otherwise silent meetings. Members are appointed to take on various responsibilities such as Elders, Overseers and Clerks, but these are rotating positions, and there is no such thing as ordination for life. Quakers thus take literally "the priesthood of all believers". Whether they are cleansed of "the madness of enthusiasm" is a moot point, to be discussed below. Like Locke, Kant would probably have applied this disparaging label to the early Quakers, but present-day British Quakers tend to be very sober in deportment and modest in their claims!

Kant distinguished between his conception of a "universal church" founded on plain rational faith, and the "ecclesiastical" or "historical faiths", i.e. the various religious traditions of the world, including the non-Christian religions. But he admitted that "due to a peculiar weakness of human nature, pure faith can never be relied upon as much as it deserves, that is, [enough] to found a Church on it alone"

(6:103). A church "needs a public form of obligation, some ecclesiastical form that depends on experiential conditions and is intrinsically contingent" (6:105, 109, 133, 192). So "ecclesiastical faith naturally precedes pure religious faith" historically, though morally it should be the other way round (6:106). Thus Kant said "there is only one (true) religion; but there can be several kinds of faith" (6:108), "different and equally good forms" of church, differing in what is inessential (6:168, 175n). He envisaged the historical faiths becoming conscious of their contingency, and gradually transforming themselves closer to pure religious faith (6:115). "The leading-string of holy tradition, with its appendages, its statutes and observances, which in its time did good service, becomes bit by bit dispensable", and "the degrading distinction between laity and clergy ceases" (6:121-2).

Quakers have their own idiosyncracies (and terminology) arising from their history, but their practice can perhaps be seen as closer to Kant's "pure religious faith" than that of many Christian churches or non-Christian religions. A statement from 1928 expresses the spirit of Quaker "Meetings for Worship":

> In silence, without rite or symbol, we have known the spirit of Christ so convincingly present in our quiet meetings that his grace dispels our faithlessness, our unwillingness, our fears, and sets our hearts aflame with the joy of adoration. We have felt the power of the Spirit renewing and recreating our love and friendship for all our fellows. This is our Eucharist and our Communion. (QFP 26.15)

In Kant's view, the purpose of all historical faiths with their claimed revelations and holy books is "to make better human beings"; so such faiths—including the (Christian) revelation, which as he rather subversively puts it "we happen to have"—should be interpreted in a way that is consistent with "the universal practical rules of a pure religion of reason" (6:110, 162, 181-2). He suggests (with danger of being patronizing) that the doctrine of revelation can be cherished as a means for presenting natural religion to "the ignorant" (6:165), and that the sacred scriptures should be interpreted as expressing moral truths about the human condition, even if this is not their literal meaning (6:83-4, 110).

Until the 20th century, Quakers quoted the Bible freely and thought of themselves as Christians, albeit of an unconventional kind. But now the position of British liberal Quakerism has considerably loosened the connection. *Advices and Queries* 4 says "The Religious Society of Friends is rooted in Christianity and has always found inspiration in the life and teachings of Jesus", but there is no mention of the doctrine of the divinity of Christ. Quakers have looked to the New Testament for illumination (as we have seen in the case of George Fox), but it is not now seen as uniquely authoritative: *Advices and Queries* 5 advises Quakers to "remember the importance of the Bible, the writings of Friends, and all writings which reveal the ways of God" (note how all three are packaged together). *Advices and Queries* 7 reads: "There is inspiration to be found all around us, in the natural world, in the sciences and arts, in our work and friendships, in our sorrows as well as in our joys. Are you open to new light, from whatever source it may come?" (There is the source of the title of this book.) This openness of approach makes it easier for Quakers to empathize with other religions, and *Advices and Queries* 6 positively recommends this: "While remaining faithful to Quaker insights, try to enter imaginatively into the life and witness of other communities of faith."

The two centuries since Kant's time can hardly be said to show very much progress towards the universal, rational kind of religion he envisioned. The resurgence of fundamentalism in several religions would surely pain him. At one point he pessimistically wrote that people's heads, "filled with dogmas of faith, have been made almost incapable of receiving the religion of reason" (6:162). However there has also been a spiritual searching for new forms of religious or quasi-religious faith and practice, manifest both in long-established groups such as Quakers and Unitarians, and in a variety of new age movements. Kant would not I think give up hope, and nor I suggest should we.

How far do Quakers and Kant agree on theology?

In the *Critique of Pure Reason* Kant criticized all the putative theoretical proofs of the existence of God, and in the *Critique of Practical Reason* he offered instead moral grounds for belief in God and an afterlife. His idea was that we need to be able to hope that God will eventually see to it that happiness is made proportionate to virtue, if we are to be motivated to keep on trying to be virtuous (these arguments have themselves come in for criticism). But it is in the *Religion* that Kant dealt most fully with religious questions. Here (especially in the First and Second parts) he treats of good and evil in human nature, forgiveness, justification and grace, scripture, revelation and history, religious mysteries and prayer, and the role of churches, ritual and priests. His language is technical, his sentences are often tortuous, and he adds footnotes of monstrous length—but he is dealing with the most profound issues of human life in an original, thought-provoking manner.

He begins by analysing what he calls the "radical evil" in human nature, namely the preference for one's own happiness over one's obligations to other people. He acknowledges the "frailty" of our nature, i.e. our difficulty in doing what we know we ought to do, and our "impurity", i.e. our tendency to confuse or adulterate moral reasons with other motives. But for Kant, what is radically evil is not so much our naturally-given needs and desires, nor the tension between them and duty, but what he labels the "depravity" of human nature, i.e. our selfishness, our freely-chosen *subordination* of duty to inclination, our constant tendency to prefer our own wants over those of others (6:19-32).

But do we really have freewill to choose between good and evil? On this point Kant, along with so many other thinkers since Augustine, is pulled in two directions. On the one hand he insists that the evil in us is a result of our own choice, our wrong use of our freedom; and in his moral philosophy he was a rock-solid defender of human freewill, even in the face of apparent determinism in the material world. But on the other hand (in his version of the doctrine of original sin), he acknowledges that evil is "radical" or innate in us, it is a universal and unavoidable feature of our condition as needy but rational beings:

> There is in the human being a natural propensity to evil; and this propensity itself is morally evil, since it must ultimately be sought in a free power of choice, and hence is imputable. This evil is *radical*, since it corrupts the ground of all maxims; as natural propensity, it is also not to be *extirpated* through human forces ... Yet it must equally be possible to *overcome* this evil, for it is found in the human being as acting freely. (6:37)

Some Enlightenment thinkers can be accused of a naïve and unrealistic optimism about human nature, but not Kant, for he is vividly aware of our potentiality for selfishness and evil, and he presents his analysis as confirming the truth behind the doctrine of original sin.

Quakers have not been very keen on the notion of sin. Their favourite phrase "that of God in every person" is sometimes taken to mean the innate goodness of human nature, but I suggest it is better interpreted as implying that we all have a *potential* for good, and are *capable* of receiving divine illumination (we are "made in the image of God", as *Genesis* puts it). But that is perfectly compatible with saying that we also have a potential for *evil*, and even an innate tendency towards it. Quakers have been aware, like most of us, of how we fall short of our high calling:

> I am conscious of a power of choice, of a better and a worse. This "ought" is my insignia of personality. Directly I admit that my life might be better than it is I have a sense of failure and feel a need of help from something or someone outside myself. This sense and this need are to me the meanings of the terms "sense of sin" and "need of salvation". (QFP 26.10)

If, as Kant wrote, the evil in us cannot be "extirpated through human forces" (6:37), Christians will be quick to insist that only God's salvation achieved through the death of Christ can suffice. Part Two of the *Religion*, entitled "The battle of the good against the evil principle for dominion over the human being", addresses these specifically Christian claims. Kant argues that the figure of Satan is a personification of the evil principle in human nature, which "makes intuitive, for practical use, the concept of something unfathomable" (6:59–60). And he treats Christ as an analogous personification of the good principle, i.e. humanity in its full moral perfection, a prototype that we can say *symbolically* "has come down from heaven, like a Son of God". But he sees no need for an actual historical exemplification of the ideal of perfection, since "the idea is present as model already in our reason" (6:62); he thus doubts the dogma of incarnation, if taken literally.

> It is easy to see, once we divest of its mystical cover this vivid mode of representing things, apparently also the only one at the time *suited to the common people*, why it (its spirit and rational meaning) has been valid and binding practically, for the whole world and at all times; because it lies near enough to every human being for each to recognize his duty in it. Its meaning is that there is absolutely no salvation for human beings except in the innermost adoption of genuine moral principles in their disposition ... (6:83)

It sounds as if Kant is endorsing the Pelagian heresy (which was fiercely resisted by Augustine and Luther) that we can only work out our own salvation by using our freewill to make the right choices; and he thereby seems to be rejecting the Christian doctrine of Christ's atoning work. But as we will see below, Kant also makes some reference to divine grace: he is a philosopher who is always trying to hold apparently opposed insight together in one big picture.

About God and immortality, Kant's attitude in the *Religion* seems rather less definite than the moral faith he had argued for in the *Critique of Practical Reason*:

> ... with respect to the object towards which our morally legislative reason bids us work, what is presupposed is an assertoric faith, practical and hence free, that promises a result for the final end of religion, and this faith needs only *the idea of God* ... without pretending to secure objective reality for it through theoretical cognition. Subjectively, the minimum of cognition (it is possible that there is a God) must alone suffice for what can be made the duty of every human being. (6:154, footnote).

Apparently all that he now thinks needed is an agnostic allowance that God *may* exist, only dogmatic atheism would be ruled out. As for life after death:

> ... glimpses into either a blessed or a cursed eternity—these are representations powerful enough ... without any necessity to presuppose *dogmatically*, as an item of doctrine, that an eternity of good or evil is the human lot also objectively: with supposed cognitions and assertions of this sort reason simply transgresses the limitations of its insight. (6:69)

So the "minimum of cognition" required for Kantian religion seems to amount to an "as if" sort of attitude: that it is good for us to behave *as if* we believe that God exists and that there is an afterlife.

Quakerism has not usually involved such highly intellectual inquiry into the philosophical foundations of morality and religious faith. But there is a corresponding emphasis on the practical character of true religion. Quakers have traditionally opposed the tendency to formulate the essence of faith in the articles of a creed, and to use it as a test of Christian orthodoxy. The *Advices and Queries* carries some authority for Quakers, but it is an expression of spirituality, practice and ethics, rather than a set of propositional beliefs. Quakers agree with Kant in asserting the primary importance of good life-conduct; but they emphasize how this depends on spiritual experience traditionally described as experience of God, or the Light of Christ, or the Holy Spirit. How far Kant could go along with that, we will examine in the next section.

The practical nature of Quaker spirituality has been well expressed by Harvey Gillman:

> For a Quaker, religion is not an external activity, concerning a special "holy" part of the self. It is an openness to the world in the here and now with the whole of the self. If this is not simply a pious commonplace, it must take into account the whole of our humanity: our attitudes to other human beings in our most intimate as well as social and political relationships. It must also take account of our life in the world around us, the way we live, the way we treat animals and the environment. In short, to put it in traditional language, there is no part of ourselves and of our relationships where God is not present. (QFP 20.20)

The Quaker suspicion of creeds was defended in a statement by London Yearly Meeting in 1917:

> We do not in the least deprecate the attempt, which must be made, since man is a rational being, to formulate intellectually the ideas which are implicit in religious experience ... But it should always be recognized that all such attempts are provisional, and can never be assumed to possess the finality of ultimate truth. ... Among the dangers of formulated statements of belief are these:
>
> a. they tend to crystallize thought on matters that will always be beyond any final embodiment in human language;
>
> b. they fetter the search for truth and for its more adequate expression;
>
> c. they set up a fence which tends to keep out of the Christian fold many sincere and seeking souls who would gladly enter it. (QFP 7.23)

Note how closely clauses (a) and (b) relate to Kant's views that theological claims lie beyond the limits of human knowledge, that all our cognition of God is merely symbolic, and that our very conception of God is "always in danger of being thought by us anthropomorphically and hence in a manner often directly prejudicial to our ethical principles" (6:182–3). Clause (c) can also be related to Kant's view that the "ecclesiastical faiths" add non-essential extras to the pure religion of reason.

A more positive defence of the Quaker attitude was offered by the astronomer Arthur Eddington in 1929:

> Rejection of creed is not inconsistent with being possessed by a living belief. We have no creed in science, but we are not lukewarm in our

> beliefs. The belief is not that all the knowledge of the universe that we hold so enthusiastically will survive in the letter; but a sureness that we are on the road. ...
>
> So too in religion we are repelled by that confident theological doctrine which has settled for all generations just how the spiritual world is worked; but we need not turn aside from the measure of light that comes into our experience showing us a Way. ... There is a kind of sureness that is very different from cocksureness. (QFP 27.24)

In its confidence in experiential method rather than intellectual doctrine, and its repudiation of "cocksureness", this is very much in the spirit of Kant's rejection of theoretical knowledge of propositions of metaphysical theology in favour of practical moral faith, involving a measured degree of hope.

Like Kant, Quakers have not insisted on the doctrine of incarnation, i.e. the metaphysical identification of Jesus with God (or at least with one Person of the Trinitarian Godhead). Consider this statement by L. Hugh Doncaster:

> The heart of the Quaker message does not lie in a doctrine expressed in abstract terms, but in an experience of power and grace, known in our hearts and also related to the structure of the universe; also known individually and recognized as belonging to all. At the same time this universal spirit is focused and made personal in Jesus in a way which makes it appropriate to speak of the Universal Light as the Light of Christ. ... (QFP 26.43)

The practical example set by Jesus was emphasized by Kathleen Lonsdale:

> To me, being a Christian is a particular way of life, not the unquestioning acceptance of a particular system of theology, not belief in the literal truth of the Virgin birth, or the Resurrection and Ascension, but being the kind of person that Jesus wanted his followers to be and doing the things he told them to do ... Nor, it seems to me, can you live a Christian life unless, like Jesus, you believe in the power of goodness, of justice, of mercy and of love. (QFP 20.26)

Does this simply reduce religion to morality? At 6:7 Kant contrasts respect for the moral law with the attitude of *worship* for the object of religion, and in the lengthy footnote at 6:6–7 he says that human beings seek something they can *love*, whereas the moral law inspires only respect. His point seems to be that if we are to find the power to live up to the demands of morality, we need to relate ourselves to something more than the moral demands themselves, and in a way that involves something like love. (Remember the distinction between questions 1–3 and 4–6 in chapter 1, and the Judaic and Christian commandment to love *God* before love of neighbour.) We need a transformation of heart and mind that remains ultimately mysterious to us; as Kant says: "how it is possible that a naturally evil human being should make himself into a good human being surpasses every concept of ours" (6:44–5). At this point he seems to allow that we have to depend on "supernatural cooperation", i.e. divine grace:

> ... the command that we ought to become better human beings still resounds unabated in our souls; consequently, we must also be capable of it, even if what we can do is of itself insufficient and, by virtue of it, we make ourselves receptive to a higher assistance inscrutable to us. (6:45)

> ... that a human being should become not merely legally good, but morally good (pleasing to God) ... cannot be effected through gradual reform but must rather be effected through a revolution in the disposition of the human being ... so a "new man" can come about only though a kind of rebirth ... and a change of heart. (6:47)

But Kant does not subscribe to an orthodox theological account of God's saving work in Christ. His philosophical position remains that we cannot *know* any such transcendent claim, and that we should not *rely* on God to transform us, without any effort on our part:

> According to moral religion ... it is a fundamental principle that, to become a better human being, everyone must do as much as it is in his powers to do; and only then ... can he hope that what does not lie in his power will be made good by cooperation from above. (6:51–2)

Later on he wrote: "true religion is not to be placed in the knowledge or the profession of what God does or has done for our salvation, but in what we must do to become worthy of it" (6:133). Yet he admits there are mysteries here that we cannot understand (6:142–4). We may *hope* for divine grace, but it is an illusion to think that we can distinguish the effects of grace from those of nature, i.e. purely human virtue (6:45, 52–3, 174, 191), for human beings are notoriously prone to self-deception (6:51, 63, 68). And we cannot induce grace through any kind of religious cult or ritual; the very idea of a "means of grace", a *technique* for achieving holiness, is self-contradictory (6:51, 174, 192–200). In that, Kant is faithful to the Lutheran Reformation.

An account of the required change of heart, also close to the words of the New Testament, but concentrating on spiritual change rather than any metaphysical theology of atonement, was given by John Wilhelm Rountree (a leaders of the liberal tendency in British Quakerism in the early 20th century):

> In Jesus, in his life and his death upon the cross, we are shown the nature of God and the possibilities that are within our reach. We are shown the world as the Father sees it, are called to live in harmony with his will and purpose, to hate the sins that made him mourn, to scale the barrier of sin and discover that the way of penitence lies open and direct to the Fatherly heart. No legal bargain, but a spiritual conflict, and inward change, the rejection of the living death of sin, the choice of new birth, of the purified self, the conversion from a low and earthly to a high and spiritual standard of life—here you have the practical conditions of salvation. (QFP 26.49)

Do Kant and Quakers differ on the possibility of religious experience?

There remains an important issue on which Quakers may appear to differ sharply from Kant. Like Locke before him, Kant expressed hostility to "enthusiastic" claims to direct experiential knowledge of God:

> ... a delusion is called enthusiastic when the imagined means themselves, being supersensible, are not within the human being's power ... this feeling of the immediate presence of the highest being, and the distinguishing of it from any other, even from the moral feeling, would constitute the receptivity of an intuition for which there is no sense [faculty] in human nature. (6:175).

'Intuition' is the traditional English translation of Kant's word *Anschauung*, which means perceptual or quasi-perceptual awareness—so Kant was here ruling out any such awareness of God. This is confirmed in one of his last publications:

> ... we would have to prove that we have had a supernatural experience, and this is a contradiction in terms. The most that could be granted is that the human being has experienced a change in himself (new and better volitions, for example) which he does not know how to explain

> except by a miracle and so by something supernatural. ... To claim that we feel as such the immediate influence of God is self-contradictory, because the idea of God lies only in reason. (*The Conflict of the Faculties* 7:57–8)

Here Kant's rather dogmatic claim is that human nature cannot contain any faculty for experience of the supernatural.

Yet the Quaker *Advices and Queries* tell its readers to "treasure your experience of God, however it comes to you" (no. 2), to "set aside times of quiet for openness to the Holy Spirit" and to "find a way into silence which allows us to deepen our awareness of the divine" (no. 3). Moreover, a Quaker meeting is supposed to enable a collective experience of the divine: "when we join with others in expectant waiting we may discover a deeper sense of God's presence" (no. 8). The experience of a "gathered" Quaker meeting has been described as a group mystical experience.

Could Kant have had a blindspot here? Could the great philosopher have missed something in the experience of many non-intellectual people?—that is possible, even the greatest thinkers have their limitations. However, there are deep problems about the description of "religious experience". Such experiences tend to be very tradition-specific, unlike our everyday concepts of material objects. (A Muslim or Jew is unlikely to have a vision of the cross or of the Virgin Mary, for example.) And there is ongoing controversy both within and between traditions about the application of religious concepts to experience. Some of the disputes are "first-order", between believers who are not prepared to accept as veridical every "inspiration from God" that others in the same tradition may claim to have—as the long history of heresy-hunting bears witness. And philosophers raise "second-order" problems about what could ever *count* as experience of something supernatural or transcendent; and the denial of its possibility is a common response, apparently exemplified by Kant.

However Kant does not deny that we can have deeply significant experiences—in *some* sense of the term—which involve awareness of some aspect of things that transcends ordinary perception or scientific knowledge. There is a much-quoted sentence at the end of his second *Critique*:

> Two things fill the mind with every new and increasing admiration and reverence, the more often and more steadily one reflects on them: the starry heavens above me and the moral law within me. (*Critique of Practical Reason* 5:161)

At the end of one of his early scientific works the youthful Kant penned a lesser-known passage expressing a kind of nature mysticism:

> In the universal quiet of nature and in the tranquility of mind there speaks the hidden capacity for knowledge of the immortal soul in unspecific language and offers undeveloped concepts that can be grasped but not described. (*Universal Natural History and Theory of the Heavens*)

In his third *Critique* Kant philosophized at length about our experience of beauty, and some of what he says there invokes a transcendent dimension to aesthetic experience, especially in his discussion of the sublime:

> ... nothing that can be an object of the senses is to be called sublime. What happens is that our imagination strives to progress towards infinity, while our reason demands absolute totality as a real idea, and so the imagination, our power of estimating the magnitude of things in the world of sense, is inadequate to that idea. Yet this inadequacy itself is the arousal in us of the feeling that we have within ourselves a supersensible power ... (*Critique of Judgment* 5:250)

In a section entitled 'Beauty as the Symbol of Morality' he writes, mysteriously:

> ... [aesthetic] judgment finds itself referred to something that is both in the subject himself and outside him, something that is neither nature nor freedom and yet is linked with the basis of freedom, the supersensible, in which the theoretical and the practical power are in an unknown manner combined and joined into a unity. (*Critique of Judgment* 5:353)

Of course it is tempting for the orthodox believer to identify this mysterious "supersensible" something with God, but Kant does not. While denying that there can be experience directly of the transcendent, he talks of certain experiences as *suggestive* of something transcendent.

By way of relief from Kant's philosophizing, here is a Quaker meditation on aesthetic experience and its relation to God written by Caroline C. Graveson:

> There is a daily round for beauty as well as for goodness, a world of flowers and books and cinemas and clothes and manners as well as of mountains and masterpieces ... God is in all beauty, not only in the natural beauty of earth and sky, but in all fitness of language and rhythm ... in all fitness of line and colour and shade ... in all fitness of

sound and beat and measure ... The quantity of God, so to speak, varies in the different examples, but His quality of beauty in fitness remains the same. (QFP 21.28)

I suggest that what is meant here is that there can be an *indirect* experience of God through the experience of beauty. It is not that God is one experienced item amongst others (not even a *specially* beautiful item!), but rather that all beauty, whether natural or manmade, can be seen as indirectly revelatory of God. In similar vein, the distinguished American Quaker Rufus Jones wrote:

> ... beauty has no function, no utility. Its value is intrinsic, not extrinsic. It is its own excuse for being. It greases no wheels, it bakes no puddings. It is a gift of sheer grace, a gratuitous largesse. It must imply behind things a Spirit that enjoys beauty for its own sake and floods the world everywhere with it. Wherever it can break through, it does break through, and our joy in it shows that we are in some sense kindred to the giver and revealer of it. (QFP 26.32)

The latter way of putting may suggest an argument from the premise that we find and enjoy beauty in the world to a proposed explanation of it as brought about by a transcendent Spirit which also enjoys it. That would be a quasi-scientific inference to the best explanation, and would lay itself open to scepticism about its reasonableness; whereas the previous passage suggests a way of feeling or thinking which is more immediately involved in the perception of beauty itself, a kind of seeing-as which is not a matter of questionable inference, but something better expressed in nature poetry such as that of Wordsworth or Gerard Manley Hopkins.

An account of religious experience by the Quaker philosopher John Macmurray in 1967 is, I suggest, consistent with Kant's sense of the depths of human experience:

> Whenever we are driven into the depths of our own being, or seek them of our own will, we are faced with a tremendous contrast. On the one side we recognize the pathetic littleness of our ephemeral existence, with no point or meaning in itself. On the other side, in the depth, there is something eternal and infinite in which our existence, and indeed all existence is grounded. This experience of the depths of existence fills us with a sense both of reverence and of responsibility, which gives even to our finite lives a meaning and a power which they do not possess in themselves. This, I am assured, is our human experience of God. (QFP 26.11)

But many people these days will want to protest: "Why do you have to drag in this antiquated and controversial God-talk?" Isn't it enough to talk of the depths of human existence? I will try to address this issue in the next chapter.

Further Reading

Most of this chapter has been adapted, with permission of the publishers, from my article "Kant's Approach to Religion compared with Quakerism", in *Kant and the New Philosophy of Religion*, ed. Chris L. Firestone & Stephen R. Palmquist (Bloomington: Indiana University Press, 2006).

For an extremely short introduction to Kant's philosophy see the relevant chapter in my book *Twelve Theories of Human Nature* 6th edition (New York: Oxford University Press 2012). For a less short introduction see Roger Scruton, *Kant* (Oxford University Press).

Peter Byrne, *Kant on God* (Aldershot: Ashgate 2007), is a fine exposition and critical evaluation of Kant's religious thought.

Most of the Kant references in this chapter are from *Religion within the Boundaries of Mere Reason*, with page references to Vol. 6 of the German Akademy edition of Kant's works. The translation is by George di Giovanni, in *Immanuel Kant, Religion and Rational Theology* (Cambridge University Press 1996); and there is also a paperback reprint of this, with a critical introduction by Robert M. Adams from a more orthodox Christian point of view.

I have used "QFP" to abbreviate *Quaker Faith and Practice*: The book of Christian discipline of the Yearly Meeting of the Religious Society of Friends (Quakers) in Britain, in the edition published by them in 1995.

I have recently published a set of essays on Kant's theoretical philosophy, *Inspirations from Kant* (New York: Oxford University Press 2011), some of which touch on issues of faith and freewill.

CHAPTER 9
GOD AS METAPHOR

Is it a matter of existence?

A book like this cannot avoid questions about God, and the various conceptions of God that are around—so here goes! Most public debate tends to assume that the most basic and important question in religion is whether God *exists*. And that is treated as if it is a question of fact about the existence of a very peculiar entity. Grammatically, it sounds like that—like the questions whether there is (or was) a Loch Ness Monster, a dark-age warrior king called Arthur, the Higgs boson, a cause of the Big Bang, or a square root of –1. Moreover the question whether God exists seems to require a clear yes-or-no answer—or at least an agnostic "don't know", where it is still assumed that there must be a definite answer, even if unknown to the speaker.

I suggest, however, that the grammatical appearances are misleading. For a start, there are competing conceptions of God. Within the monotheistic Judeo-Christian-Islamic tradition, ideas of the divine have varied widely over the centuries; and differences between tribal or universal, punishing or forgiving, timeless or changing, personal or impersonal, Trinitarian and non-Trinitarian conceptions of God are still around today. It is not clear that all Christians share the same concept of God—let alone Jews and Muslims, or adherents of other religions. The question "Does God exist?" is thus as ambiguous as the concept of God itself, so if one is challenged to say whether one believes in God, it is quite reasonable to reply "If you tell me what *you mean* by 'God', I'll tell you if I believe in *that*"! Equally, those who proclaim they don't believe in God can be asked what *sort* of God it is that they don't believe in.

Given a certain conception of God, rooted in one of the various traditions of religious practice, I am going to argue that the question whether one believes in that sort of God can be taken as asking how illuminating one finds that family of theistic figures of speech in thinking about life, and how committed one is to participating in the relevant tradition in one's own spiritual journey. Answers to *these* questions can, quite reasonably, be not yes-or-no but a matter of *degree*, for what is involved is more the a matter of commitment to a tradition of figurative language and spiritual practice than of finding evidence for a scientific hypothesis or arguing by pure reason for a metaphysical speculation.

This approach may offer some defence of the tendency of many Quakers, when pressed to say what they actually *believe*, to react with some hesitation and embarrassment. The questions are sometimes put: *What* do you worship in your so-called "Meetings for Worship"? If you talk of "the will of God" and of "divine" Light or inspiration, surely you believe in God? The evasive reply may well be "Some of us do, some of us don't", or "It all depends on what you mean by 'God'". More positively, however, a recent booklet *Twelve Quakers and God* reveals an interesting variety of views: "absolute love, total goodness ... a power which is beyond me and is too great for my complete apprehension, yet is part of me, and of all others"; "a reality that cannot be named ... a warmth, a real presence in my life ... a disturbing one, too"; "a force ... within me and outside me, omnipresent in the world"; "a power to be drawn on and from which to receive strength"; "good energy will always be there"; "the life-force ... Being, unlimited by time or space ... purpose ... a presence in my heart and in my bowels ... a guiding force in my life"; "the power, the love, the challenge, that I call God"; "the song of the Spirit is everywhere ... I lay down God as noun, and take up the Spirit as verb"; "my God is not just personal; S/he is also power or energy, the Divine Source"; "I have never really been sure about God ... sometimes I think I am verging on being atheist ... one place where I feel God most strongly in Quaker meetings for worship"; "I use many names for the Divine ... I want to express my awe before the greatness of God, but have not-yet-found the vocabulary"; "what I worship ... is the fundamental Energy of on-going creation ... the ever-present Energy is there to be drawn on by anyone who opens himself or herself to it".

There is a vagueness here (some might say confusion or incoherence!) about what exactly we are talking about, and how it (or He? or She?) should be described. Yet there is in almost all these cases a tested confidence, a deeply-held faith, that some version or other of this long-inherited and multi-faceted God-talk, for all its difficulties and unclarities, expresses something that is in *some* way real, and of fundamental importance for our lives. In the following historical and philosophical reflections, I would like to defend this vague but real faith against both the strident atheists on one side and the dogmatic theologians and philosophers of religions on the other.

Conceptions of God in the Bible and the *Qur'an*

Let us go back to the beginnings of monotheism, and consider how God is represented in the Hebrew Scriptures. Moses is described as talking with Him face to face as one man speaks to another, yet he was afraid to look at God, and was not allowed to see His face, though at one point he was allowed to glimpse His back (*Exodus* 33:23). God was thus represented as occupying a spatial location, and as having a visible, indeed a dangerous, appearance:

> The Lord came down on the top of Mount Sinai and summoned Moses up to the mountaintop.
>
> The Lord said to him, Go down; warn the people solemnly that they must not force their way through to the Lord to see him, or many of them will perish. (*Exodus* 19:20–21)

Elsewhere however, God has only a voice, with which He speaks to individuals, usually in imperative mode, as in *1 Samuel* Ch. 3 (in verse 10 He is described as "standing there"). The *Psalms* portray God very variously—as a shield, a lofty crag, as having fingers and a mouth, and famously as a shepherd in *Psalm* 23. There is also an image of God as a dragon-like creature riding through the sky:

> When in anguish of heart I cried to the Lord, and called for help to my God; he heard me from his temple, and my cry reached his ears ...
>
> Smoke went up from his nostrils, devouring fire from his mouth ... thick darkness lay under his feet.
>
> He flew on the back of a cherub: he swooped on the wings of the wind. (*Psalm* 18: 6–10)

Did the ancient Hebrews take these very physical descriptions of God literally? Perhaps some did, perhaps some didn't, or perhaps they didn't make any such distinction—and how could we ever know? How should *we* read them? Should *we* take them any differently from the stories of the Greek gods?

> As [Achilles'] racing spirit veered back and forth,
> just as he drew his huge blade from its sheath,

> down from the vaulting heavens swept Athena,
> ... Her gray eyes clear, the goddess Athena answered,
> "Down from the skies I come to check your rage
> if only you will yield ..." (Homer, *The Iliad* I: 227–243)

It is hard to know whether Homer and his audiences believed that the Greek gods literally flew down form the sky to intervene in human affairs. But when we read Homer, we will surely take these dramatic interventions of the gods as personifications of human thoughts and passions. In the quoted passage Athena can be read as the vehicle of Achilles' second thoughts, inhibiting him from acting on his anger. If we read or sing the *Psalms*, we can take the stuff about God riding on a cherub with smoke coming out of his nostrils as just a vivid visual picture of His awesome power, and the description of God as a shepherd leading the psalmist into green pastures as a poetic image of His loving care.

But where then is the dividing line between what we should take as metaphorical or literal? The *Psalms* also speak of God getting angry, hearing weeping, reviving people's spirits and guiding them on the right paths. These are things that a human being can quite literally be said to do, though answering prayers and passing judgment on the nations (*Psalm* 9:5) may be a bit much to expect even of the most powerful human ruler. Some will say that if we think of God as a disembodied *person*, He can be conceived as having such thoughts and feelings (and perhaps actions). But how can there be divine perceptions without divine sense-organs? And a disembodied God's thoughts, emotions and actions would have to occur without the bodily expressions which typify them in humans. So if God enjoys such mental states at all, they would have to be inconceivably different from what they are in us.

In the *Proverbs*, wisdom is personified as a female figure in the very same passage as the Lord of Hosts, provoking the question whether the latter is any less of a personification than the former:

> Happy is he who has found wisdom ...
> She is more precious than red coral ...
> In her right hand is long life; in her left are riches and honour ...
> By wisdom the Lord laid the earth's foundations, and by understanding
> he set the heavens in place. (*Proverbs* 3: 13–19)

(Some scholars may detect here an alien intrusion of Greek thought into the otherwise purely monotheist Hebrew Scriptures.)

In the New Testament, Jesus's talk of God as "Father", and his instruction to us to pray to Him as "Father", is clearly metaphorical; the Christian God is not conceived of as fathering children on mortal women in the fashion of some of the Greek gods. Christians who say that Jesus was the Son of God do not believe *that*, as is indicated by that mysterious credal phrase "conceived by the Holy Ghost". As we saw in Chapter 3, many of the parables in Jesus's teaching are extended metaphors or analogies, implicitly comparing God with a landlord, a shepherd, a sower of seed, etc., and leaving it to the hearers and readers to puzzle out the spiritual meaning of each parable.

At various places in the New Testament, however, some physical-sounding divine actions are reported: a divine voice speaks from heaven and the Holy Spirit descends in the form of a dove (*Mark* 1:10–11), Jesus is said to have ascended into the sky (*Acts* 1:9–11), and Paul told the early Christians that they would meet Jesus in the clouds at the second coming (*1 Thessalonians* 4:17). The early compilers and readers of the New Testament may have taken these things literally. But most of the writing of St. Paul is at a spiritual level: for instance, he cannot have meant it literally when he said that he had himself been crucified:

> I have been crucified with Christ; the life I now live is not my life, but the life which Christ lives in me; and my present mortal life is lived by faith in the Son of God, who loved me, and gave himself up for me. (*Galatians* 2:20)

Paul was under no illusion that he himself had been nailed to a cross, or that the human Jesus lived on inside his body in some extraordinary parasitic manner; he obviously had a metaphorical spiritual meaning in mind when he wrote those words—which raises interesting questions about how to interpret the rest of Paul's writing. In contrast, the last book of the Christian Bible deploys a phantasmagoria of apocalyptic imagery, including God sitting on a throne (*Revelation* 4:10–11), where it seems we have come full circle back to the physically-embodied God of *Exodus*, which is inconsistent with *1 John* 4:12 (supposedly the same author) declaring that no-one has seen God.

In the *Qur'an*, as far as I know, no such bodily imagery is used of God. The accounts of the afterlife, with the Fire and its torments for evildoers and the Garden and its sensuous delights for the righteous, are indeed almost grossly physical (e.g. 3:131–136, and Suras 55–56). (One can readily understand how for desert-dwellers, a well-watered fruitful garden would be an image of bliss. And some recent Islamic accounts of heavenly reward have encouraged male sexual fantasies.)

But the God of the *Qur'an* remains supremely transcendent of all such physical description. More than once, it is insisted (against the Christians) that He is far above fathering a son:

> Say [Prophet], "If the Lord of mercy [truly] had offspring I would be the first to worship [them], but—exalted be the Lord of the heavens and earth, the lord of the Throne—He is far above their false descriptions." (43:81–2; see also 10:68, 19:35)

It would be interesting to hear from Muslim scholars whether they reject only the idea of God *literally* fathering a son (which is not, of course, what Christians believe), or whether they mean to rule out any metaphorical use of the phrase "Son of God".

Personification in the arts

In the developing Christian tradition, there was wide use of iconography, especially in the Eastern Orthodox Church, focusing very much on the figure of Christ, but sometimes depicting the Trinity rather literal-mindedly as three angelic persons. Later on, Western artists painted God as a bearded white male of a certain age, thereby exerting a stranglehold over our visual imagination that persists to the present day, when people ridicule the idea of an old man in the sky. In Michelangelo's painting of God fingertipping Adam into existence the Creator appears to have the same size, shape and solidity (and race and gender) as Adam; the touch of fingers is a symmetrical relation, but creation surely cannot be. Wittgenstein wrote about that picture: "If we ever saw this, we certainly wouldn't think this the Deity. The picture has to be used in an entirely different way if we are to call the man in that queer blanket 'God'"(*Lectures and Conversations on Aesthetics, Psychology and Religious Belief*, p. 63). William Blake painted God as a naked old man with a flowing white beard streaming in the wind, deploying a mathematical instrument in the process of creation. Publishers still insist on recycling these images on the front covers of books, even when the actual content of the book radically undercuts belief in them (for example, *God, Jesus and Belief* by Stewart Sutherland).

Theologians will protest that such paintings are mere pictorial images, and that anyone who thinks *that* is the sort of God the tradition believes in is missing the point. But then why invite the misunderstanding so dramatically? We may feel some sympathy with the Mosaic ban on graven images, and the Islamic rejection of representational art in religion, perhaps even with the iconoclasm that divided Christian Byzantium in the 8th and 9th centuries (though since then Eastern Orthodoxy has positively revelled in icons).

We surely have to take William Blake's much-reprinted etching of an aging hippy wielding a slide-rule in the process of creation just as non-literally as his personifying poem *To Spring*:

> O Thou with dewy locks, who lookest down
> Through the clear windows of the morning, turn
> Thine angel eyes upon our western isle,
> Which in full choir hails thy approach, O Spring! ...
>
> Come o'er the eastern hills, and let our winds
> Kiss thy perfumed garments; let us taste
> Thy morn and evening breath; scatter thy pearls
> Upon our lovesick land that mourns for thee.
>
> O deck her forth with thy fair fingers; pour
> The soft kisses on her bosom; and put
> Thy golden crown upon her languish'd head,
> Whose modest tresses are bound up for thee.

It used to be a convention in much poetry and art to personify all sorts of abstract ideas. There are paintings of "Virtue" as a buxom female of a certain size sailing about somewhat awkwardly in the sky, with a cherub larking about under her ample skirts (Tiepelo, *The Triumph of Virtue and Nobility over Ignorance*) — but much work of this period now tends to excite sniggers and derision more than aesthetic or spiritual appreciation. Still, Blake's personification of Spring as a longed-for, returning lover can be enjoyed as a poetic *jeu d'ésprit*. And it is after all about *something* real, for the coming of spring is a real event with wonderful effects on all living things, and Blake uses his imagery to express that wonder.

Personification in theology

Are there any limits to metaphor and personification in theistic thought and language, then? Many believers want to draw a line in the theological sand, and insist that *some* talk of God must be taken literally as implying a metaphysical proposition about the existence of an infinite personal Being, with the traditional attributes of omnipotence, omniscience and perfect benevolence. They will readily admit that the religious emphasis should be on the *attitudes* of faith in God and obedience to Him, but they will point out, plausibly enough, that such attitudes seem to presuppose the existence of a personal Being to whom they are to be directed. As *Hebrews* 11:6 puts it: "whoever comes to God must believe that He exists".

Most debate, both at the popular and the academic level, has thus assumed that talk of God has to be interpreted as implying the existence of a superhuman person. Since He is not now thought of as having a physical body, it is often said that we have to think of God as a *dis*embodied person, with the infinite properties of omniscience, omnipotence, and total benevolence. Many philosophers of religion take this conception for granted, and conduct all their discussion on that assumption. For example, Richard Swinburne's weighty trilogy of books on the concept and existence of God deploys the conceptual machinery of modern philosophy of science and theory of probability in the (to my mind, misguided) effort to show that belief in God is justified as the best explanation of all the observed facts. The conception he assumes at the outset is that God is, quite literally:

> ... a person without a body (i.e. a spirit) who is eternal, free, able to do anything, knows everything, is perfectly good, is the proper object of human worship and obedience, the creator and sustainer of the universe. (R. Swinburne, *The Coherence of Theism*, Oxford University Press 1977, p. 1)

On the other side of the Atlantic, Alvin Plantinga has written another massive trilogy of books, deploying all the sophistication of late 20th century epistemology to the quite opposite conclusion that Christian belief does not *need* empirical justification, and can quite reasonably be taken as "basic", i.e. as something Christians are rationally entitled to accept without having to offer *evidence* for it. But like Swinburne, Plantinga assumes the same metaphysical conception of God at the very beginning:

> God is a person; that is, a being with intellect and will ... God is thus all-knowing and all-powerful; he is also perfectly good and wholly loving. Still further, he has created the universe and constantly upholds and providentially guides it. (A. Plantinga, *Warranted Christian Belief*, Oxford University Press 2000, Preface)

But there are other philosophers and theologians who explicitly reject the assumption that God is, quite literally, a supernormal person; for example Sallie McFague:

> A genuinely metaphorical theology ... recognizes the limitations of *all* models and abjures a "super model", such as the personal one is often assumed to be in [the Judeo-Christian] tradition. God is not a "person" or "personal" as such; this model does not cease to be a metaphor merely because it is a more inclusive model than many others in the tradition. (S. McFague, *Metaphorical Theology: Models of God in Religious Language*, SCM Press 1982, p. 128)

Nicholas Lash also rejects the common premise of the ambitious intellectual constructions by Swinburne and Plantinga:

> We address God as "you", and speak of God as "him", rather than "it", not because God is "a person" (which he certainly is not, for he is not an anything), but because our Christian experience of the manner of God's action requires us to acknowledge ourselves to be not merely produced but addressed, not merely made but loved, and speaking and loving are *personal* characteristics. (N. Lash, *Easter in Ordinary: Reflections on Human Experience and the Knowledge of God*, SCM Press 1988, p. 276)

When some of our most distinguished theologians and philosophers of religion disagree on such fundamental points as whether God is a person, and on whether belief in Him stands in need of evidence, one is tempted to think that the concept of God is not in terribly good shape! Peter Byrne concludes that theology, unlike science, cannot be construed as a realist discipline, for it has no agreed methodology for settling disputes, and has made no discernible progress over two thousand years; theology, in his view, shows no signs of being controlled by an object external to itself. (Peter Byrne, *God and Realism*, Ch. 7). I will touch below on the question whether the outlook for theology is quite so bleak.

God-talk without personification

Lash's words quoted above may seem open to an obvious riposte from the theological realist: *who* then is doing this "addressing" and "loving"? If such experience is not illusory, surely Lash's description of it as "our Christian experience of the manner of God's action" implies the existence of a supernormal person after all? The reply Lash must surely give is to say that all this talk of God's action, speech and love which comes so naturally to those brought up in the Biblical tradition is just as metaphorical as the more physical talk of God we have sampled. On this view, these personifications are tradition-sanctioned figures of speech by which we try to express something real, but which transcends ordinary personality. Thus we can take talk of God as an overarching picture or metaphor (or perhaps, a model or recipe for generating many metaphors). God-talk has provided a system of imagery which many have found illuminating and inspiring in understanding and coping with their experience of life—its ups and downs, its delights and disasters, loves and hates, successes and failures, forgiveness, illuminations, and creative new possibilities.

It may be some relief to realize that what we are considering is not a new problem, but the classic dilemma of all theology—trying to use words to express things that are ultimately beyond all words. The mysterious 4th–5th century writer known as "the Pseudo-Dionysius" is reported as saying that man cannot understand the names of God. As we saw in Chapter 5, Origen amongst the church fathers and Ibn Sina and Ibn Rushd amongst the Muslims and the great Jewish philosopher Maimonides all argued that the language of popular religion is metaphorical, and cannot be taken literally by philosophers.

Mystics such as the Jewish Zohar, the Islamic Sufis, and the Christian Meister Eckhardt have strained language to breaking point in trying to communicate their experience:

> You should love Him as he is: a non-God, a non-spirit, a non-person, a non-image; rather as He is a sheer pure limpid One, detached from all duality. And in that One may we eternally sink from nothingness to nothingness. So help us God. Amen. (Eckhardt, *Sermons and Treatises*, p. 335)

(Eckhardt wrote of God in such negative-sounding and paradoxical terms that at the end of his life he was summoned by the Inquisition, and though he died before he could appear before them, he was posthumously found guilty of error.) According to both Aquinas and Kant (two very different philosophers from the 13th and 18th centuries), all our talk of God is analogical. Quakers have emphasized religious experience over creeds.

But the crusading atheist may still want to force the issue: "Come on now: do you, or do you not, mean to say that the whole history of the universe is the act of a disembodied super-person, with the purpose of maximizing personal freedom, creativity and love? Or is this just a fanciful picture, a poetic image, a fairy-tale which you recommend that we entertain without really believing it, since encouraging the growth of freedom, creativity and love is such a worthy aim, and entertaining that picture in our minds may (so you say) help us further it in practice?"

On the other side, the traditionalist theologian, voicing the feelings of fundamentalist believers, may protest: "You are in danger of reducing belief in God to the adoption of moral ideals, and of claimed means for furthering them. But if you abandon the metaphysical foundation of belief in a God who really acts in creation, revelation and redemption, and in providentially guiding human history towards its ultimate fulfillment, you will lose both the intelligibility of the traditional words you want to continue to utter, and the distinctive faith and hope offered by the Christian gospel."

Both critics assume a robustly—but perhaps *naïvely*—realist interpretation of religious language, as opposed to the anti-realism or reductionism they would diagnose in the approach I am favouring. As we have seen in our historical survey in Chapter 5, there is a constant tendency for religious thought and debate to return (often, it seems, with a certain relief!) to seemingly clear and hard-line traditional positions. But the danger is that such polarized sides will learn nothing, because they are unwilling to recognize anything that does not conform to their own prejudices.

Is there a way to weave between the horns of the above dilemma, using the concept of metaphor? I suggest that both the crusading atheist and the fundamentalist believer are being unduly literal-minded when they interpret religious talk as making *quasi-scientific* truth-claims about the world. If we are to see the gradual emergence of our world as a divine act with an overall purpose to maximize the growth of personal freedom, creativity and love—need we be forced to choose between interpreting that as edifying fiction or as literal truth? Can't we say that this is a word-picture or elaborate set of metaphors involving the notions of intention and love applied on a cosmic scale, which expresses some of the most fundamental realities that we experience in life—though not literally, and certainly not scientifically? Isn't there such a thing as *poetic* truth? And isn't that a guide to the kind of truth, if any, that we can expect in religion and theology?

Farrer on poetic truth

Some seventy years ago, Austin Farrer penned an inspirational paper entitled "Poetic Truth". He set out to explore whether the metaphorical language which is characteristic of so much poetry may "throw some light on the way in which we have to think about the soul and about

God". He argued that although figurative poetry can "speak straight to the heart" more than plain prose, it is quite wrong to conclude that all that metaphor does is to convey or arouse emotion:

> Do you really think that such writing never illuminates the real object which the poet is professing to describe? Do you think that from reading or hearing such poetry you never come away with a livelier sense of what exists, exists not in your heart in the poet's heart, but out there in the world which is his and yours? (p. 27)

Thus Farrer declares that to read a poet like A.E. Housman is not just to find out how he reacted to certain aspects of human destiny, but "to apprehend more strongly ... man's position in the universe and setting in the context of inhuman nature". So metaphor is not only the language of emotion, but of description:

> And we say that it is good and true when it effectively describes what the poet sees, whether he is looking at his own heart, or his own dream, or the real world of things, or a mixture of them all. (p. 29)

Metaphor, Farrer argues, is often the best means of description because it does not analyse in the way that science does, rather it tries to express the individual character of things. In poetry—and in love—we are driven to metaphor, not just to express our emotion, but to describe its object. But is any such "poetic truth" possible in theology? Farrer was a robust theist, a theological realist if ever there was one, who combined deep spirituality in the high Anglican tradition with immense learning and a delightful writing style. On religious language, his position was recognizably descendent from Aquinas:

> If metaphor and comparison can really illuminate, it must be because the things compared are really alike in the required respect. Behind metaphors stands real analogy. (p. 32)

> It is therefore not a scandal, but something every hearer of poetry should understand, that all the statements we make about God are similitudes, as it is written, *per speculum in enigmate* ['Through a glass darkly']. (p. 35)

Realism, however, is an elusive philosophical concept that takes on different guises in different contexts. Farrer's theological realism may need some elucidation and qualification. He rated both God and the soul as real existents that stand in need of approximate, metaphorical description:

GOD AS METAPHOR

> Of all things known to us, the most simply and absolutely unique is God; and next to him, the human soul. The soul is not much like anything else, and so men have always been forced to talk about it in unconvincing metaphors: a flame of inspiration, a force of will, a weighing-scale of choice... (pp. 33-4)

Indeed, when you think about it, much of our everyday language about our states of mind—or soul, if you will—can be recognized as metaphorical, though perhaps Farrer over-reached himself in suggesting that *all* such metaphors are unconvincing. For instance, the common phrase "falling in love" is a metaphor, since involuntary downward movement through space under the force of gravity is not thereby implied! But the experience is real, and it involves an involuntary attraction to a real person outside oneself (the metaphor seems convincing enough to me). Poets have waxed lyrical—and metaphorical—about love since time immemorial. Alkaios's Greek poem from the 2nd century BCE puts it down to darts fired by the god Eros:

> I hate Eros. He is loathsome and will not
> Hunt animals, but takes my heart for a target.
> What good is it, a god inflaming a man?
> What prize to boast of will he get for my heart?
>
> Alkaios, poem no. 229 in *The Greek Anthology*, edited by Peter Jay (Penguin 1981).

There is obviously no need to take that personification literally, and I doubt if the poet himself did, he was surely just enjoying making a clever little conceit out of it.

Metaphorical as much of our talk of states of mind or soul may be, Farrer was thoroughly convinced of the reality of the soul:

> But the soul does exist: there is nothing of which we are more aware, for it is we ourselves; only its uniqueness and singleness prevents our talking prose about it, and that's the whole of the mystery. (p. 34)

But when he affirms so resolutely that the soul *exists*, what is it that he thereby asserts? The word "soul" comes trailing a long and tangled history of controversial folk-belief, theology and philosophy. It carries connotations of an entity that is immaterial, yet carries the essential identity and moral responsibility of an individual person, and is believed to survive into an afterlife and indeed to be immortal (Plato's *Phaedo* is a classic text). But for anyone who has been impressed by

Hume's argument that the self is not an object of experience, or by the Paralogisms section of Kant's *Critique of Pure Reason*, or by Buddhist arguments that the self is an illusion, these metaphysical assertions about the soul are deeply controversial. They can hardly be said to be simply given in introspection, or straightforwardly provable by analysis of the concept of a person or the use of the first-person pronoun.

Farrer knew a thing or two about philosophy, but he did not call Hume or Kant to mind at this point. What then did he think was so obvious about saying that the soul exists? I hazard the guess that it is the existence of *persons*, and all the manifold states of mind that we can have as persons. Amongst these are states of cognition (beliefs, guesses, inquiries, knowledge), emotional states (erotic love, hate, anger, fear, jealousy, pride, etc.), and—as Farrer would obviously emphasize— those states that, although they involve the emotions, also invite the adjective "spiritual" (regret, guilt, despair, humility, hope, forgiveness, unselfish love, etc). Whatever our religion or culture, our theology or philosophy, we can all agree that there are such states, and that they are crucially important in our lives. After all, we each experience most of them for ourselves. In this uncontentious sense, we all have souls (or minds—if you prefer that term).

Farrer apparently hoped that he could take the reality of God to be just as evident as that of states of soul:

> God is a reality as is our soul, absolutely present and active in the existence and operation of all the creatures; for they are the expression of continual creative power. (p. 35)

But what we said about the word "soul" applies in spades to the word "God", for it too comes trailing a long and tangled history of controversial folklore, theology and philosophy. We noted at the beginning of this chapter that there are different conceptions of God, so it is not clear what Farrer is entitled to affirm as so *obviously* real here. Of course he wanted to affirm the God of long-standing Christian tradition; but the reality of God, thus conceived, is notoriously far from evident to everyone. Is there anything corresponding to God-talk that we can uncontentiously affirm to be real, in the way that we can affirm states of mind or soul as experienced realities while avoiding philosophical controversy about the nature of the soul?

Metaphorical realism in theology?

Here I would like to offer a suggestion. Consider the word "life" in its widest possible usage (perhaps dignified with a capital L), referring not just to all living things, but to "Life" as that of which we sometimes portentously discuss "the Meaning". We complain and suffer, and sometimes despair, about the difficulties and disasters that Life throws at us; in more fortunate times we may exult in and give thanks for the delights and fulfillments that Life offers. Looking backwards, we realize that Life has a long history: each individual person is a product of a family and a society, humans have evolved from simpler forms of life on earth by a process of natural selection, the earth itself is a product of stellar evolution, and science tells us that the story of the whole material universe goes back to the Big Bang. But when we talk of the Meaning of Life, we tend to look *forwards* to purposes and values and ideals, rather than backwards to causal, scientifically-discoverable, conditions. Life in this wide sense is ever-present, active and creative (which are words that Farrer applies to God). For Life manifestly produces human persons, in our glories—and our depravities. Amongst our glories is our sense of how we *should* be different from what we are, and amongst the greatest things that Life can offer is a sense of forgiveness for our inadequacies and wrongdoings, and inspiration and power to live more nearly up to the ideals we recognize as drawing us.

I am not proposing a synonymy between "God" and "Life". My suggestion is only that the latter word, in this admittedly vague (and indeed itself metaphorical) usage, roughly delineates the *field of discourse* into which talk of God enters as a personifying figure of speech. What I am trying to do is to mark out the ground on which theistic constructions and figures of speech may be built, the level of reality to which they refer. Quakers have come up with some similar thoughts, for example John Lampen wrote in 1985:

> To apply the term "God" in the Christian sense is to say that we perceive intuitively a connection between the marvels of the natural world, the moral law, the life of Jesus, the depths of the human personality, our imaginations about time, death and eternity, our experiences of human forgiveness and love, and the finest insights of the Christian tradition. To deny the existence of "God" is to say that we cannot (yet) see such connections. But even the word "God" is not an essential tool for grasping them. (QFP 26.33)

Rex Ambler has written:

> ... we should altogether stop talking about God as a being of some sort, an imaginable entity, whether male or female, personal or impersonal, and bring our language back to the experience and practice where it really belongs. God is part of a story we tell about ourselves in order to convey something of the depth and mystery and creative power that we experience among ourselves and that we are hoping to trust and act upon in the conduct of our lives. God is a metaphor for the kind of reality that cannot be talked about directly and literally, certainly not in scientific language, or in rational philosophy either. But it is not a metaphor that we absolutely need for experiencing and responding to the reality it is supposed to be referring to. It is after all only a word.
> Rex Ambler, *The End of words: Issues in Contemporary Quaker Theology* (London: Quaker Home Service 1994), pp. 24–5.

That sounds very reductionist, especially in that last throw-away line, but note that Ambler is still saying that there is a *reality* of some sort that talk of God is trying to express. There is, however, some sloppiness here in the failure to distinguish God from the concept of God, and even from the word 'God', so I would suggest rewriting the passage as follows:

> The "surface grammar" of talk about God is reference to a conscious being of some sort—usually a disembodied (yet male!) person. But if we interpret this theological language in terms of our actual experience and practice, we find that its "depth grammar" is rather different. The concept of God is part of a story or theory or interpretative scheme we tell in order to convey something of the depth and mystery and creative power that we experience among ourselves and in the universe and that we are hoping to trust and act upon in the conduct of our lives. The concept of God is a metaphor for this kind of reality, which cannot be adequately described by scientific theory or in metaphysical philosophy either. Yet the time-hallowed monotheist language-game of God-talk is not absolutely compulsory for experiencing and responding to the reality it is supposed to be referring to; other traditions use different figures of speech for the same purpose.

But while suggesting that the concept of God is optional, though distinctive of the Western religious tradition, this Quaker emphasis remains on the experience of "spiritual reality". There is a recognition of what has traditionally been called "the presence of God", together with an awareness that language is inadequate to fully and literally express what we are trying to talk about here. An eloquent recent passage by Beth Allen uses rather more of the traditional Christian language:

> By "God" I mean the energy flowing through all the created universe, beyond us all and yet at the same time giving God's nature to be known — transcendent yet immanent, loving yet full of truth, eternal, outside time yet working in time, the source of all that is, yet incarnate, given particular voice and form in Jesus yet also a light within every person, a powerful transforming Spirit, fluid, elusive, which is also a still small voice asking for our co-operation in cherishing real overflowing abundant life in every single thing.
>
> Because of this, we can be held securely and confidently in our deepest being.
>
> Beth Allen, Ground and Spring: Foundations of Quaker Discipleship (London, Quaker Books 2007), p. 113.

Other religious and non-religious discussions of the meaning of life and how to live it wisely also tend to use metaphorical talk of their own — for example the newly-popular (often Buddhist-derived) meditation techniques or therapies of "Mindfulness". It would be an interesting exercise to explore how much commonality lies beneath the differences of language. Here is an alternative vocabulary used by Vaclav Hawel, writing when he was a leader of the civil resistance to the last stage of communist rule in Czechoslovakia:

> At the basis of this world are values which are simply there, perennially, before we ever speak of them, before we reflect upon them and enquire about them. It owes its internal coherence to something like a "pre-speculative" assumption that the world functions and is generally possible at all only because there is something beyond its horizon, something beyond or above it that might escape our understanding and our grasp but, for just that reason, firmly grounds this world, bestows upon it its order and measure, and is the hidden source of all the rules, customs, commandments, prohibitions ... Any attempt to spurn it, master it, or replace it with something else, appears, within the framework of the natural world, as an expression of *hubris* for which humans must pay a heavy price. (V. Havel, *Living in Truth*, ed. Jan Vadislav, Faber & Faber 1989, pp. 137–8)

Many readers of this passage will immediately identify this transcendent "something" with God. But there is an alternative that Havel himself may have preferred, namely Plato's form of the Good (see Chapter 4). Iris Murdoch sang its praises some time ago (in *The Sovereignty of Good*), and in her last philosophical work before she descended into Alzheimer's she offered a radical reinterpretation of the traditional Ontological Proof of the existence of God as a meditation on "the fundamental and omnipresent (uniquely necessary) nature of moral value, thought of in a Christian context as God" (*Metaphysics as a Guide to Morals*, Ch.13).

At this point, perhaps there is a little more to say about realism. According to a criterion for reality that goes as far back as Plato (*The Sophist* 247E), what is real must stand in causal relations, and in particular it must have real effects. This readily applies to states of mind or soul, for they have undeniably real effects for good or ill—such as marriages and murders, poetry and wars. But does this test apply to God? To treat God as a mere personification may seem to make Him just a figure of speech, and totally unreal, whereas traditional conceptions of God think of Him as the Creator of the whole universe. Moreover many believers hold that God can be, and has been, the cause or agent (in some more specific sense) of many particular events within it, and He has been looked to in hope, as the Providential Guide of the whole history of the universe towards its eventual fulfillment.

It would take a lengthy book to discuss in what sense, if any, God can be said to act in the world; and of course there are many such books already (not least one by Austin Farrer—*Faith and Speculation* 1967). All I can do here is to indicate that the all-embracing loose talk of Life that I have been indulging in above allows plenty of leg-room for causes and effects. The immensely long processes of evolution of life on earth have produced the human species, and we depend for our continued individual and collective existence on many biological, economic and ecological processes outside ourselves. We are strongly influenced by our society, and especially these days by the media, and the culture and fashions they ubiquitously purvey. But, despite appearances, we are not totally determined in our ideas and behaviour by all that stuff: there remains room for choice, freewill, or "inspiration"—a word whose etymology involves the breathing in of "spirit" or "Spirit", perhaps something divine. To put it metaphorically, as one inevitably does with these matters, chinks of

Light can be discerned in the darkness. When people act on their vision of the Light, real effects can ensue in human lives.

But of course, none of this implies that all figures of speech are equally *appropriate*, whether in literature or in religion or anywhere else. Not all poetry is much good: that is painfully apparent to producers and consumers of the stuff, and there is an industry of literary criticism to explain why. Metaphors and figures of speech that are effective in one era and culture may not be in another age or another society, at least not without special efforts at interpretation. The figurative language of popular devotion and of much theology is meant to express experienced spiritual realities, above all the ever-present possibility of spiritual regeneration and transformation. But not all of it is equally edifying, though to some extent what is preferred will be a matter of taste and fashion. Many hymns recycle monarchical and ceremonial imagery about God and the afterlife, and have lost effect in our less metaphysical and deferential age. Fortunately there are plenty of alternative images available, from the Bible and elsewhere. Talk of divine "illuminations" and "leadings" is less grossly physical, and has deep roots in many traditions, before Quakers and since.

I suggested at the beginning of this chapter that the question whether one believes in God can be taken as asking how illuminating one finds theistic figures of speech in one's spiritual journey. On this view, belief in God is rather more like belief in homeopathy, psychoanalysis, or cold showers than belief in the Loch Ness monster. As Wittgenstein said:

> If the question arises as to the existence of a god or God, it plays an entirely different role to that of the existence of any person or object I ever heard of. (*Lectures and Conversations on Aesthetics, Psychology and Religious Belief*, p. 59).

> ... what is important is not the *words* you use or what you think while saying them, so much as the difference that they make at different points of life. How do I know that two people mean the same thing when each says he believes in God? And just the same thing goes for the Trinity. Theology that insists on *certain* words and phrases and prohibits others makes nothing clearer.

> It gesticulates with words, as it were, because it wants to say something and does not know how to express it. *Practice* gives the words their sense. (*Culture and Value*, revised edition, p. 97)

What is involved here is a commitment to a way of life rather than wavering belief in the existence of a possibly-mythical entity (Kant described it as *faith* rather than *opinion*). But this usually involves some combination of theory and practice. If one is willing to undergo a treatment or participate in some supposedly therapeutic procedure, that is because one hopes for beneficial effects from it, so one had better have some degree of confidence that the assumptions on which it is based are true, or at least approximately right. Of course, one may try out a therapy on no stronger evidence than the recommendation of a friend, or in desperation; but if it makes people feel better, it must have some sort of relation to reality, even if only through the placebo effect, which is real in its own way. There may be rival theoretical beliefs about it; there are different schools of thought within psychoanalysis, and for all I know within homeopathy too—and there notoriously are in religion and theology! Sometimes we know *that* a practice works without knowing *how* it works. In that connection, recall the saying "By their fruits shall ye know them".

Here is another striking passage from Wittgenstein's remarks on life, culture, and religion:

> It appears to me as though a religious belief could only be (something like) passionately committing oneself to a system of coordinates. Hence although it's belief, it is really a way of living, or a way of judging life. Passionately taking up this interpretation. (*Culture and Value*, revised edition, p. 73)

A system of mathematical coordinates is not a common object of passionate commitment, but Wittgenstein was only suggesting a partial analogy. To try to put his point more exactly, religious commitment is to a set of concepts and beliefs for interpreting the meaning and purpose of life. These are usually handed down by tradition (new sects and cults and gurus and therapies or life-guides keep turning up, but they are usually variations on old themes). In connecting with the realities of human life, such concepts and beliefs have to relate to reality, even if indirectly. So I suggest that the use of metaphor and personification in poetic and religious language does not exclude reference—perhaps even revealing, enlightening, soul-transforming reference—to important aspects of the reality of human life; it is only an unduly literalist and unimaginative kind of realism that thinks otherwise.

Further reading

The historical development of concepts of God has been elegantly surveyed by Karen Armstrong, in *A History of God: From Abraham to the Present: the 4000-year Quest for God* (London: Heinemann 1992; Vintage 1999).

Twelve Quakers and God (Hampstead: Quaker Quest, 2004) contains the variety of views excerpted above.

Richard Swinburne's view that the existence of God is a question to be settled by the same criteria as we operate in science, history, and detective work is summarized in his short book *Is There a God?* (Oxford University Press 1996).

Gareth Moore, a member of the Dominican Order of Preachers, has offered an interpretation of Christian talk of God strongly based on Wittgenstein's philosophy in *Believing in God* (Edinburgh: T&T Clark 1988). This is more interesting than the rather conventional title suggests, for it is an extended (if somewhat longwinded) argument that "God" is not the name of a person who does things, and that religious language is not in the business of offering causal explanations.

Ludwig Wittgenstein's remarks about religion are found in his *Lectures and Conversations on Aesthetics, Psychology and Religious Belief* (Oxford: Blackwell 1966), and in *Culture and Value: A Selection from the Posthumous Remains*, Revised second edition (Oxford: Blackwell 1998).

The conceptual problems about God are elegantly presented by Peter Vardy, in *The Puzzle of God* (London: HarperCollins, revised edition 1995); by Keith Ward (with a delightful sense of humour) in *God: A Guide for the Perplexed* (Oxford: Oneworld 2002); and with philosophical sophistication by Peter Byrne, in *God and Realism* (Aldershot: Ashgate 2003).

Austin Farrer's paper "Poetic Truth" was discovered amongst his manuscripts and posthumously published in A. Farrer, *Reflective Faith*, ed. Charles Conti (London: SPCK 1972); the editor dates this paper to the 1940s.

The claim that metaphorical language can express certain kinds of truth, especially in religion, has been reinforced by many recent writers:

Sally McFague, *Metaphorical Theology: Models of God in Religious Language* (London: SCM Press 1982);

Leszek Kolakowski, *Religion* (St. Augustine's Press 1982), Ch.5;

Janet Martin Soskice, *Metaphor and Religious Language* (Oxford University Press 1985), Ch.VI–VIII;

T.R. Wright, *Theology and Literature* (Oxford: Blackwell 1988), Ch. 1;

Iris Murdoch, *Metaphysics as a Guide to Morals* (London: Chatto & Windus 1992);

Paul Avis, *God and the Creative Imagination: Metaphor, Symbol and Myth in Religion and Theology* (London: Routledge 1999);

John Cottingham, *The Spiritual Dimension* (Oxford University Press 2005), Ch. 5;

Vincent Brummer, *Vincent Brummer on Meaning and the Christian Faith* (Aldershot: Ashgate 2006), Ch. 4.13.

Colin Gunton, in *The Actuality of Atonement: A Study of Metaphor, Rationality and the Christian Tradition* (London: T&T Clark Ltd: 1988), makes a sophisticated defence of the use of metaphor in theology, and an exploration of three families of metaphor that have been used to explain the cosmic significance of Christ's death on the cross.

Stewart Sutherland's book *God, Jesus and Belief* (Oxford: Blackwell 1984) is more exciting than its conventional-sounding title suggests, for he suggests some radical revisions of Christian belief about God, and about Jesus.

In my essay "Twelve Conceptions of Imagination" in the *British Journal of Aesthetics* 2003, I suggest towards the end that there is a kind of imaginative grasp of deep truths about life that is both argued for and exemplified in Wordsworth's great autobiographical poem *The Prelude*.

CHAPTER 10
RESURRECTION?

Dogma and openness in religion

The three Semitic religions each refer back in history to a particular claimed divine revelation that they recognize as uniquely authoritative. Jews trace their status as "God's chosen people" right back to the deliverance of the children of Israel from slavery in Egypt a thousand years or more before Christ, their passage through the wilderness of Sinai under the leadership of Moses, and their conquest of "the promised land" of Canaan. Christians acknowledge those events and the subsequent history of ancient Israel as manifesting God's purposes, but find His supreme revelation of Himself in the life, death, and resurrection of Jesus, as documented in the New Testament. Muslims make some acknowledgement of most of the above (while remaining conspicuously silent about Jesus' death and alleged resurrection), but they insist that the final revelation of God is the *Qur'an*, handed down word-for-word to Muhammad.

In each case, membership of the religion is essentially defined by faithfulness to the original revelation, the contents of which become unquestioned dogma. Jewish identity consists more in practical adherence to the divine Law and rituals laid down in the Torah than in propositional belief ("ortho-praxis" rather than ortho-doxy). But the various strands of Orthodox and Reformed Jewry tend to differ vehemently amongst themselves about what counts as correct Jewish practice, and even on who counts as Jewish. Jewishness is an ethnic as well as a religious concept, but there are ethnic Jews who neither believe in God nor practise the rituals, and on the other hand those not born Jewish can convert to Judaism (which for males requires the delicate matter of circumcision). Christianity, at least from the time of Nicea onwards, has concentrated on correct belief as set out in the various creeds and "confessions", though baptism and eucharist have usually been seen as compulsory as well. But as we have seen in

Chapter 5, theological views have divided and diversified, and some Christian authorities have been prepared to persecute, torture and burn those they saw as heretics. Muslims simplified things to the "five pillars" of Islam: *shahada*, or profession of faith; *salat*, or daily worship; *zakat*, or almsgiving; *ramadan*, the annual fast; and the *hajj*, or pilgrimage to Mecca. The *shahad* seems very simple—"There is no god but God, and Muhammad is his messenger"—but it commits the believer to accepting that the *Qur'an* is the final revelation of divine truth on all things. As for other world religions, I must leave it to those who know them better to say how far they define themselves in terms of loyalty to an ancient tradition. (Buddhism has recently offered some doctrine-free practical advice on how to achieve peace of mind and happiness, in the form of books by the Dalai Lama and others; but some versions of Buddhism invoke controversial metaphysical beliefs about reincarnation of the same individual through a succession of lives, and "karma", i.e. the moral effects of one such life upon another.)

There is surely a large element of social psychology, sociology and politics in these matters of defining religious membership. People typically want badges of group identity, whether tribal, national, religious, or sporting (and sometimes several of these are confused or combined). For better or for worse, religion still has power over large numbers of people, as even the most dogmatic of atheists have to admit. Churches and religions can exert strong influence on society and politics; as we have seen, they have traditionally been part of the power structure. The Catholic Church dominated the medieval history of Europe, and the Reformation made an enormous social and political difference to Europe thereafter. Judaism is part of the definition of the modern state of Israel. Islam has dominated the culture of many countries in the Middle East, North Africa, and beyond; in contemporary Iran, the Shi'ite version of Islam exercises supreme political leadership. Anyone proposing a different version of religious belief or membership from that which prevails can be seen as a threat to the religious or political power of those presently regarded as authoritative. This explains but does not excuse the frequent resort to violence; in societies where that has thankfully receded, a residual *"odium theologicum"* has often characterized theological differences, unlike scientific or philosophical debates.

But does it *have* to be like this? Must all religious belief and practice rest on fundamental dogmas that are held beyond all rational discussion and scrutiny? Does every form of religions require a blind,

RESURRECTION?

unquestioned commitment to an ancient revelation (or rather, the presently-authoritative interpretation of it)? The whole trend of this book is to say: surely not. Quakerism, at least in its British liberal version, is a counter-example. It has its own distinctive tradition, looking back to the insights of George Fox, but not uniquely to him (and he is certainly not regarded as infallible). The Quaker way is explicitly open to new insights from other traditions, and from new guidance of the Spirit. *Advices and Queries* 4–7 read as follows:

4. The Religious Society of Friends is rooted in Christianity and has always found inspiration in the life and teachings of Jesus. How do you interpret your faith in the light of this heritage? How does Jesus speak to you today? Are you following Jesus' example of love in action? Are you learning from his life the reality and cost of obedience? How does his relationship with God challenge and inspire you?

5. Take time to learn about other people's experiences of the Light. Remember the importance of the Bible, the writings of Friends and all writings which reveal the ways of God. As you learn from others, can you in turn give freely from what you have gained? While respecting the experiences and opinions of others, do not be afraid to say what you have found and what you value. Appreciate that doubt and questioning can also lead to spiritual growth and to a greater awareness of the Light that is within us all.

6. Do you work gladly with other religious groups in the pursuit of common goals? While remaining faithful to Quaker insights, try to enter imaginatively into the life and witness of other communities of faith, creating together the bonds of friendship.

7. Be aware of the spirit of God at work in the ordinary activities and experience of your daily life. Spiritual learning continues throughout life, and often in unexpected ways. There is inspiration to be found all around us, in the natural worlds, in the science and arts, in our work and friendships, in our sorrows as well as in our joys. Are you open to new light, form whatever source it may come? Do you approach new ideas with discernment?

Of course Quakers can be challenged as to what they really believe. But such questions need to be directed to individuals, for there is no

Quaker creed that defines membership, only a willingness to join in the spiritual way of life that is expressed in *Advices and Queries* and other Quaker writings.

In the previous chapter I outlined a non-literal approach to the use of "God"-language, which still allowed that such language is talking, figuratively, about some aspects of the reality of human life. In this chapter I will attempt something similar for talk of resurrection. I have hesitated about doing this, for beliefs and hopes about an afterlife have been precious to many people and central to many traditions, above all to Christianity; and just about every possible theological position has already been occupied, in many cases long ago. But in a book like this I can hardly duck the topic, so in the spirit of the Quaker quotations above I will explore what Christians have believed about resurrection and what is thought to be so important about it, while not feeling committed in advance to accepting any particular view.

What is resurrection of the body supposed to be?

Judaism in Jesus's time had begun to develop a belief in a general resurrection, at some time in the distant future, of the righteous dead to a new divinely-given kind of life, though this was denied by the party of the Sadducees. Christianity took over this belief, but added the completely new idea that Jesus had been individually resurrected, ahead of time, on the third day after his death. The Christian belief is in the resurrection of *the body* (as the creeds say); and the scriptural warrant for this consists in the reports at the end of the gospels of Jesus's visible and tangible re-appearances, and Paul's writing in *1 Corinthians* 15 that we die as physical bodies but are raised as "spiritual bodies". Paul did not explain what a spiritual body is supposed to be, but he did use the Greek word *soma*, which means body. The Christian claim was thus crucially different from the Greek idea of the survival of an incorporeal soul, although the Platonic (or Cartesian) concept of a non-material and potentially disembodied soul has entered into much Christian thought and language down the centuries, with the result that there has been considerable unclarity and confusion on the nature of life after death.

The Christian doctrine of the afterlife as embodied seems consistent even with a thoroughly materialist view of human nature, since the bodies we are supposed to have in the afterlife must presumably be made of matter of some sort. It seems to fit even better with Aristotle's view (which we looked at in Chapter 4) of the mind or soul as the way that the living body and brain function. Perhaps the distinctive way of functioning (the software) can be instantiated in a new body (hardware). As we saw in Chapter 5, Aquinas tried to integrate Christianity with Aristotle on human nature, though with a bit of backsliding towards the Platonic view of incorporeal soul.

Jewish beliefs about life after death also seem to have wavered between these two quite different understandings. They have sometimes been combined into a two-stage theory, with the incorporeal soul waiting around after death, until fitted out with a new body in the general resurrection, which seems to have been Aquinas's considered view. The *Qur'an* has a lot to say about the afterlife, mostly in very literal bodily terms involving intense pleasures or pains; thus it too involves some conception of bodily resurrection. However the great Muslim philosophers ibn Sina and ibn Rushd doubted the literal truth of bodily resurrection, as also did Maimonides the medieval Jewish philosopher (as we saw in Chapter 5). I am going to focus on this belief in *resurrected bodies* that is common to the three Abrahamic religions (even if they are not entirely consistent about it). I will first explore its meaning and its difficulties in the general case, before looking at the special case of Jesus. And I will voice some sceptical thoughts before suggesting anything more positive.

A normal human body consists of a highly-organized collection of matter, occupying a certain portion of space, and living for some length of time, after which there is decay or destruction. A resurrected body, if it is to be a *body* at all, must presumably also consist of organized matter occupying space and time—though the usual understanding is that its endurance in time is infinitely extended, with no further possibility of death. It seems we thus have to imagine a whole resurrection world, usually called "heaven" (plus hell?) or "God's space", containing living human bodies—and presumably animals, plants, and inanimate objects, too. But, despite Dante's very detailed descriptions of the spatial structure of hell, purgatory, and heaven in his 14th-century *Divine Comedy*, it is not now believed that somewhere in our physical universe, perhaps at some enormous distance from the earth beyond all possibility of investigation by us, there are to be found the resurrected bodies of St. Augustine, Charles I (with head restored?), and great-aunt Agatha. That would make the belief into a scientific hypothesis—though getting evidence for it might prove difficult. In a more metaphysical interpretation, the resurrection world can be understood to occupy a different sort of space and time which bears no spatial or temporal relations with our world. But on a rather different eschatological interpretation, heaven (and hell?) is said to be what will become of *our* world, *in our space*, when God re-creates it at the end of ordinary time.

In all these accounts of the resurrection we are said to be given new life, so the resurrection body is definitely supposed to be *alive*. But is this biological life? Is there metabolism—eating, digestion, and excretion? Is there sexuality and reproduction? Presumably the orthodox Christian answer is "no", since Jesus is recorded as saying that in the resurrection people are not married or given in marriage (*Mark* 12:18–27, *Matthew* 22:23–33, *Luke* 20:27–40). It is sometimes said that our resurrection bodies will be incorruptible: but how can they be *alive*, without being vulnerable to illness and disease, accidents and injuries, and death? Are there bodily sensations (painful and pleasurable)? Is there perception, involving causation from things in the resurrection world to eyes, ears and skin, and thence to the brain and conscious awareness? Is there action, involving causation from thoughts and intentions via bodily movements to effects in the resurrection world?

The resurrection life is obviously supposed to be a life of *persons*. There must therefore be time and change, and personal interaction. (If it is said that the resurrection world exists in timeless eternity, how can there be personal relationships without communication and interaction?) Will personal relations continue to be mediated by speech, gesture, facial expression, touch and embrace? Will we remain young, middle-aged or old, according to our age at time of death? Even if our new bodies are ageless, will we remain youthful, mature, or elderly in our attitudes and character? Will we be sexed? Even if our resurrection bodies are made sexless, will we remain male and female (and heterosexual or homosexual) in our psychology and in the ways we relate to each other? Can old relationships be renewed, and new ones formed? Can they be disrupted? (Does nothing ever go wrong?)

Personal relationships can involve growth in mutual understanding and love, but there is no guarantee of this. As we all know, other people can be difficult to cope with, in many ways, and we ourselves can fail. No doubt we would hope that heaven will be different: well, it may be better, but can it be different in principle? Isn't there bound to be some possibility of misunderstanding, puzzlement, disappointment, annoyance, and blame? One hopes that a measure of tolerance and forgiveness will enable us to leave behind much of this, but it doesn't always happen smoothly. Misunderstandings can grow into resentment, long-term enmity or obsessive hatred. Of course we are attracted by descriptions of a heavenly life in which all is sweetness and light. But—at the risk of seeming churlish in criticizing people's conceptions of heaven—can we coherently picture all that white light without even the *possibility* of some darker colours?

The resurrection has always been supposed to be of the *same individuals* who lived and died on earth, and who are now given a new (or renewed) body. Unless personal identity is thus preserved beyond death, the whole conception of a resurrection world is of no more interest than the idea of biologically-functioning replicas of our bodies being created elsewhere in the universe. (And the same point applies to the Eastern idea of the same person being reincarnated in a new body, again and again.) But what constitutes the identity of persons across death? It cannot consist in continuity of matter: there is no need to think, gruesomely, of bones and decaying flesh being literally raised out of graves. In many cases not even bones remain: and I understand that cremation, or burial at sea, or "sky-burial" (being eaten by vultures) are not now thought of as preventing resurrection. It may be suggested that an omnipotent God could re-assemble all the atoms that constituted my body at the moment of my death, but even that would not be sufficient to make such a re-assembly *me*, rather than a copy of me. Sameness of matter is not necessary to personal identity anyway, for our bodies do not contain the same matter through ordinary life, because of our continual metabolism.

Memories of one's life on earth must surely be preserved if we are to speak of the same person being resurrected. But do the resurrected people have to carry on from the physical and mental state and memories they had at the time of death? For many, that would imply being resurrected in a very reduced state, and in Alzheimer's cases the memories may be almost completely erased. Resurrection on those terms is hardly attractive. If it is suggested that we should take up our resurrected life at the height of our powers, as it were, by what criteria is that "height" to be selected, and how could our subsequent earthly history be passed over while preserving our personal identities? Someone might advance in spirituality while declining physically, and the reverse is also possible. For those who die in infancy or childhood, resurrection hardly seems attractive unless they could make mental and spiritual progress from there in the new life.

Presumably the resurrection life must involve decision, choice, and responsibility for one's actions, for how could it be the continued life of a *person* unless there is freewill in this broad sense? But if it does, then it surely follows that things can grow worse as well as better in the resurrection world, just as they do in this world: there could be minor tiffs, major suffering and even evil. (I am thinking primarily of *mental* hurts and suffering here, which must surely be possible even if physical pain could be ruled out.) Bishop Tom Wright says "Forget all those stories about lounging around playing harps — there will be work to be done", which seems wise, for humankind cannot bear too much leisure. But work implies putting effort into achieving something, and if we are persons at all we will surely retain some choice and responsibility for how much attention and effort we put into our tasks in the resurrection world. What we try to do may not always happen, otherwise it wouldn't be *work*! It seems that the more we try to make sense of the hypothesis of the life of persons continuing in a world of resurrected bodies, the more we have to reduplicate the fundamental features of personal life in this world — good, bad and indifferent.

If we think of the resurrected life not as timeless, but as a life that literally goes on for ever, is that really an attractive prospect? The answer is, I suggest, not obvious. Could life remain meaningful if we knew there could be no end to it? Inter-generational relationships are vital in parenting, and welcome in grand-parenting, but could we cope with endless numbers of ancestors and descendents? And what on earth (or rather, in heaven!) would people do with all that endless time? Some depictions of heaven are in danger of sounding like a high-class hotel in which all one's needs are discreetly catered for, and there is plenty of congenial company to chat to — very pleasant too, as an interlude of relaxation, consumption and conviviality in a life that contains work, political commitments, bringing up children, and anything else that demands physical or mental effort. But as an everlasting life, surely its sweetness would soon cloy, and it could turn into hell, as Sartre envisaged in his play *Huis Clos (No Exit)*.

A common response to such questions is to complain that they miss the point: we do not know in detail what the resurrected life will be like, we just have to accept it in faith. But that is to imply that we do not and cannot know *what* it is we are accepting "in faith". What seems to be going on is that we are being pressured to accept a certain form of words that has been hallowed by a particular tradition, usually going back to some ancient writings regarded as uniquely authoritative. It comes down to what the believer may describe as "a choice of worldview", or what the unbeliever may say is a matter of party loyalty: "If you're going to be a member of our tradition, you've got to accept this dogma". The choice is most fundamentally about what authority to accept for belief. Should we allow those writings that are regarded as canonical to trump everything else we think we know about the world? Or are there no "trumps" in epistemology, morality and religion, no particular sort of evidence that should always win?

Of course, there are many who quickly dismiss the whole idea of resurrection and afterlife as mere superstition, a mental hangover from ancient religion which we "mature, enlightened, scientifically-educated" moderns should have been able to get over some time ago. But I am not entirely happy with such a complacent attitude. Of course, we have learnt much about the world from science, and we have absorbed much of the moral and political ideals of the Enlightenment (in my view, quite rightly—see Chapter 7). However, human nature, individually and collectively, stubbornly retains capacities for evil as well as for good, and we cannot rely on science alone to tell us what is good, nor how to live up to it. But that does not mean that the only alternative is to opt uncritically for one or other of the various religious traditions still on the market. We can listen to what they have to say, and be prepared to learn from it, without having to commit ourselves to the *whole* package of beliefs and practice that may be pressed on us. And *within* traditions there are always questions of interpretation about how sacred scripture are to be understood, and which elements of time-hallowed practice should be carried forward. So let me now ask what we can make of the Christian tradition about Jesus's resurrection.

The resurrection of Jesus?

We noted at the beginning of Chapter 5 that the motif of a God dying and coming back to life was found in several religions or cults in the ancient world. But those beliefs have largely disappeared, while Christianity has emphasized the cosmological and spiritual importance of Jesus's resurrection and made it central to a worldwide faith over two millennia. Christians typically claim that the resurrection of Jesus was both a real observable event in history, and a unique act of God. The idea of the Virgin Birth is almost as miraculous, but though it is there in the creed it is nowadays often seen as less crucial to Christianity. (If there can be flexibility on one point, why not on another?)

Some Christians may say that I have been approaching things the wrong way round, that it is Jesus's resurrection that is supposed to show the possibility of a similar resurrection for everybody (or at least, for the righteous, "the elect"). But Jews and Muslims also believe in a general resurrection, so it is not true that nobody but Christians can accept it. Christians may reply that what happened to Jesus is the best *proof* of the reality of resurrection for everyone, so we will have to address that claim. But here we run into the difficult matter of historical claims about an alleged miraculous event two thousand years ago.

Let us be clear about what is *meant* by the resurrection of Jesus. It is not resuscitation, i.e. not that Jesus came back to life after apparently dying on the cross, lived on a bit longer, and eventually died in one of the normal ways. Resuscitation is now performed in hospitals, but I understand it has to be done pretty quickly after the stopping of the heart. Resuscitation (without technology) is presumably what Jesus is (implausibly) supposed to have done for Lazarus after four days in the tomb (*John* 11:1-45), and perhaps for Jairus's daughter (*Luke* 9:40-56) though in her case it is not made so clear that she was really dead. But it is clear that the New Testament writers did not think that Jesus was brought back to *normal* life, for the reports of his resurrection have him appearing and disappearing at will. And there are absolutely no reports of his subsequent death (in which there would surely have been intense interest) only a mysterious description of his bodily "ascent into heaven" (*Acts* 1:9).

Nor was it meant that "the resurrection" was only a set of subjective psychological/spiritual experiences on the part of Jesus's followers, though it certainly involved such experiences, and generated the conviction and energy that brought the early Christian church into existence. The gospels say that after his crucifixion, Jesus's body was put into the rocky tomb, which was later discovered to be empty, with the grave clothes left lying there. The emptiness of the tomb is supposed to be a very significant fact, for the claim is made that the matter in his corpse was somehow "used up" to constitute a new kind of "spiritual body" which was visibly recognizable as Jesus himself speaking, walking and eating, yet with a body that was able to pass through walls.

This suggests a metaphysical picture of a different order of reality ("God's space"), which briefly intersected with our ordinary world of space, time and matter in Jerusalem about 30 CE. There is also the claim that this divine order of reality will eventually break in again and bring human history to an end, with the resurrection of humans into spiritual bodies like that of the resurrected Christ. Yet in *Matthew* 27:52-3 there is a report that at the very time of Jesus's death "graves opened; many of God's saints were raised from sleep, and coming out of their graves after his resurrection entered the Holy City, where many saw them". But as far as I know, Christians have tended to pass over this passage (in embarrassment?), and have stuck to the line that the general resurrection must wait for the end of history. (I can't help wondering if the "saints" were firmly told they were jumping the gun, and were sent back into their graves to wait for the end of time! Sorry—that's a Pythonesque fantasy!)

The suggestion about matter from the corpse being "used up" to make the resurrection body invites awkward questions from scientists about conservation of matter and energy. But is it necessary to the resurrection claim? Why should the new "spiritual body" need to use the matter from the corpse? As we have already noted, our bodies do not contain the same matter through our ordinary lives. So the reported emptiness of Christ's tomb would seem to be irrelevant to the resurrection-claim, which could still be asserted even if his body remained there, decomposing in the normal way, or if his skeleton could somehow be identified even now. Even if, anachronistically, a surveillance camera showed the corpse mysteriously dissolving into thin air as in a science-fiction movie, that in itself would still not prove that Jesus was resurrected elsewhere. But in any case, I do not see how at this distance of time we can ever know whether the tomb was empty and what became of Jesus's corpse. On these questions of historical fact, the only rational response is surely agnosticism.

As for the reports of Jesus's resurrection appearances, they go beyond the assertion of the emptiness of the tomb, they involve a metaphysical claim, and hence a "choice of worldview", as noted above. For someone not already disposed to such a worldview, nothing in the historical evidence can force them to espouse it. It is an undisputable fact that the early followers of Jesus were somehow energized and inspired to proclaim his resurrection soon after his death, and to say that this implied a spiritual message of salvation to everyone. But how to *explain* this fact, and in particular whether to take the gospel accounts of Jesus's re-appearances at face value, remains deeply controversial, and I suspect that no amount of historical investigation or philosophical or theological argument is ever going to settle the argument. One is not rationally obliged to offer an alternative explanation concerning such distant and controversial historical claims, one can just maintain an attitude of agnosticism about what actually happened, and why.

Resurrection as spiritual renewal

I don't want to end on a note of scepticism and negativity (tinged with flippancy). Rather, I venture to suggest that some of the mainstream Christian talk of resurrection can be interpreted in terms of a message of spiritual renewal that does not depend on controversial historical or metaphysical dogmas. As we have seen already, a lot of Christian language is obviously metaphorical. Consider the perhaps over-used idea of being "born again". When Nicodemus came to talk to Jesus by night, Jesus tells him that no one can see the kingdom of God unless he has been born again. Nicodemus takes that crudely literally and protests that nobody can enter his mother's womb a second time, but Jesus answers:

> In very truth I tell you, no one can enter the kingdom of God without being born from water and spirit. Flesh can give birth only to flesh, it is spirit that give birth to spirit. You ought not to be astonished when I say "You must all be born again". The wind blows where it wills; you hear the sound of it, but you do not know where it comes from or where it is going. So it is with everyone who is born from the Spirit. (*John* 3:5-8)

The talk of being born from water is an obvious reference to baptism, but the idea of being "born from the Spirit" surely means a radical spiritual change. At *John* 6:63 Jesus says that it is the spirit that gives life, the flesh can achieve nothing, which implies that the ritual of baptism can only be an outward material sign of an inward spiritual process (and in the case of infant baptism, it will have to refer forward in time). At 3:16 Jesus says that whoever has faith in him will not perish but will have eternal (or everlasting) life.

But we need not jump to the conclusion that these phrases must involve the continuation of human life after death. They can mean a new and better way of living in *this* life — a way that relates properly to eternal truths and values, a Spirit-inspired, divinely-loving life in this world. Admittedly, there are other passages in the gospels (especially in *Matthew*) that lay great stress on resurrection after death, a last judgment, eternal punishment for the wicked, and everlasting life after death for all believers (e.g. *Matthew* 7:21-23, 13:36-43, and Ch.24-25), but readers will be aware by now that I am not committed to taking everything in the New Testament at face value. Paul's writings often employ metaphorical language:

> By baptism we were buried with him [Christ Jesus], and lay dead, in order that, as Christ was raised from the dead in the splendour of the Father, we also we might set our feet upon the new path of life. (*Romans* 6:4)

> So you, my friends, have died to the law by becoming identified with the body of Christ, and accordingly you have found another husband in him who rose from the dead. (*Romans* 7:4)

> Do you not know that your bodies are limbs and organs of Christ? (*1 Corinthians* 6:15)

> I have been crucified with Christ: the life I now live is not my life, but the life which Christ lives in me. (*Galatians* 2.20)

> In him [Christ] also you were circumcised, not in a physical sense, but by being divested of the lower nature. (*Colossians* 2:11)

Such quotations demonstrate beyond all doubt that Paul often uses melodramatic bodily imagery to express and illuminate the spiritual matters he is concerned with. And it seems to me that he was thus talking of the life of the resurrected Christ as a new kind of spiritual life that his believers find themselves living.

However it cannot be denied that elsewhere Paul quite literally and unambiguously asserts the reality of bodily resurrection, above all in *1 Corinthians* Ch. 15. He recounts the stories of Jesus's post-mortem apparitions, and he proclaims that belief in the resurrection of the dead is essential to the Christian faith as he understands it: "If there be no resurrection, then Christ was not raised; and if Christ was not raised, then our gospel is null and void, and so is your faith" (v. 13); "If it is for this life only that Christ has given us hope, we of all men are most to be pitied" (v. 19); "For the trumpet will sound, and the dead will rise immortal, and we shall be changed" (v. 52). I see little prospect of interpreting *these* words metaphorically—though perhaps the trumpet is optional! And the Creeds and the mainstream Christian traditions have insisted ever since that belief in Jesus's bodily resurrection is absolutely central.

We are thus faced with a choice of world-view. If we are to go along with the whole package of traditional Christianity, we are expected to believe in the bodily resurrection of Christ, and eventually of the rest of us. We will then have to find whatever maneuvers we can to make that consistent with everything else we know and believe about how the world works. But I suggest that if we are agnostic or sceptical about resurrection, *literally* interpreted, we do not have to reject Christianity *en bloc*. We can try to discern what is worth learning from the Christian tradition—and I do not mean just in an intellectual, academic way, but what we find inspiring for our lives. A spiritual interpretation of resurrection was suggested by the Quaker astronomer Jocelyn Burnell:

> The resurrection, however literally or otherwise we interpret it, demonstrates the power of God, to bring life out of brokenness; not just to take the hurt out of brokenness but to add something to the world. It helps us to sense the usefulness, the possible meaning in our suffering, and to turn it into a gift. (*Quaker Faith and Practice* 26.56)

From what you have already read in this book, you might predict that Quakers would take some such line. But I want to ask how much of the spiritual message of mainstream Christianity can be disentangled from the controversial history and metaphysics. I have found some striking quotations from Roman Catholicism, Anglicanism, and Orthodoxy.

Here is the Abbot of the Benedictine Abbey at Pluscarden in Scotland:

> 'The disciples rejoiced' (*John* 20:20). Then there's joy. We may distinguish happiness and joy. Happiness is emotional, joy is spiritual. Happiness is more external, joy more internal. Happiness is more subjective, joy more objective. Happiness is a reaction, joy is a response. Happiness is ephemeral, joy lasts. *Chairete*, Rejoice! says Jesus as he rises. The Resurrection of Jesus is joy. It is joy greater than any that has ever been or will ever be in the history of mankind. I will see you again and your hearts will rejoice, and no one will take your joy from you (*John* 16:22). The Resurrection is the irruption of God's joy in our life, the beginning of a joy that will last. ... This joy is the calm recognition of the presence of definitive salvation and ultimate good. (Dom Hugh Gilbert, *Unfolding the Mystery*, Ch. 15, p. 100)

I expect that Dom Hugh would say that his joyful yet calm conviction in salvation and ultimate good *depends* on his belief in Christ's bodily resurrection two thousand years ago, but I want to ask (with all due reverence) whether it *has* to depend that. Can't one believe, with a sense of joyful conviction, that there is always potential for good in the world, despite all the indications to the contrary, while being agnostic about such distant and mysterious historical claims?

RESURRECTION?

Next let me quote from the Archbishop of Canterbury's book on resurrection. It is difficult to select brief passages from his subtle and wordy prose, but I hope the following will not be misleading:

> *This* man and his way of living and dying, this man rather than any other, is exalted, approved and vindicated. The preaching of the resurrection takes this out of the realm of mere report by its address to a particular audience, its requirement that they see themselves as guilty of the violence of the cross and turn back to their victim. ... Thus the process begins by which the particularity of Jesus crucified and proclaimed as Saviour in Jerusalem becomes a universal symbol, the focus and pivot of a fresh and transforming interpretation of all human reality. The solidity and resourcefulness of the symbol can be ground only in the process of interpretation, not straightforwardly in historical research ... (Rowan Williams, *Resurrection*, p. 20).

> ... the Christian proclamation of the resurrection of the crucified just man, his return to his unfaithful friends and his empowering of them to forgive in his name offers a narrative structure in which we can locate our recovery of identity and human possibility; a paradigm of the "saving" process; yet not only a paradigm. It is a story which is itself an indispensable *agent* in the completion of this process ... (p. 43)

> The risen Christ is not a resuscitated human *individual*; he is encountered as a particular historical subject, certainly, in the records of past events, but the work he now performs in our lives cannot be understood in terms of what a human individual, past or present, might do. (p. 55)

> ... the apparitions have no meaning independently of the establishment of the community, so there is no reason for any interest in the detail of these encounters for their own sake. ... To see the risen Jesus is to see one's own past and one's own vocation, to "see" the call towards the new humanity. ... There is no hope of understanding resurrection outside the process of renewing humanity in forgiveness. (p. 109)

Rowan Williams offers a succession of attractive phrases which express what he sees as the spiritual meaning of Christ's resurrection: "a universal symbol, the focus and pivot of a fresh and transforming interpretation of all human reality"; "a narrative structure in which we can locate our recovery of identity and human possibility"; "to see one's own past and one's own vocation, to 'see' the call towards the new humanity". And he seems rather to downplay the importance of what may or may not have happened all those years ago, though I suspect he could not move any further in that direction without being accused of heresy (which would not be a new experience for Archbishops of Canterbury!)

Thirdly, here is a representative of Eastern Orthodoxy—the Christian tradition which has above all others emphasized the celebration of Easter with all-night vigils, the veneration of icons, and the triumphant cry "Christ is risen!"

> "No one can say: 'Jesus is Lord,' except by the Holy Spirit" (1 *Corinthians* 12:3). Without the Spirit it is impossible to believe in Christ and in His Resurrection. The example of the apostles—their disbelief, followed by their faith suddenly revived by the resurrected Christ, who sends them the Spirit in order to make them steadfast in their witness—proves that it is the Spirit Himself who resurrects. Underestimating the power of the Spirit amounts to depriving the Resurrection of Christ of its vital dynamism. Without the spirit, one inevitably objectifies the Resurrection and makes of it a mere abstraction. (Michel Quenot, *The Resurrection and the Icon*, p. 72)

> How can we hope to restore the spiritual content of the Resurrection, the Mystery of mysteries, if not through symbols? In Orthodoxy, these are not mere representations of a reality, they are themselves a manifestation of this reality. A full reading of [icons] can be made, therefore, only through the powerful symbolism that opens the soul and the heart to [their] inexhaustible hidden meaning. (p. 82)

> The Resurrection stands in direct opposition to the notion of corruption. The gates of Hell have been shattered forever. Even though nothingness and death, the forces of evil that have already been defeated, remain present for a time, creation has been freed and has found its essential meaning and its deepest unity. (p. 226)

Again, the symbolic and spiritual meaning of Christ's resurrection is strongly emphasized: without that, it is said to be "objectified" and made into a mere abstraction. But I presume that this author, along with all of Orthodoxy, would strongly resist my suggestion that the spiritual meaning can be disconnected from claims about what happened to Jesus in a particular time and place.

All three of these writers are full of joyous conviction of a deep spiritual meaning that is potentially transformative of the whole of human life. But they would almost certainly want to distance themselves from the position I am arguing for in this chapter, and they might accuse me of selective quotation. (Of course all quotation, short of repetition of the whole, is selective—the real complaint would have to be of *misleading* quotation. I can only say that I have quoted more than single sentences, and have tried not to be misleading in my selection.) I do not find that the joyous conviction has to depend either on a historical claim about what happened to one man two thousand years ago, or on a metaphysical theory about life after death.

Wittgenstein and an epistemology of love?

Amongst many striking remarks in his private jottings on life, the universe and everything, Wittgenstein wrote: "Only *love* can believe the Resurrection. Or: it is *love* that believes the Resurrection." (*Culture and Value*, revised edition, p. 39—in an entry dating from 1937). Bishop Tom Wright seizes on this as confirming the need for "an epistemology of love":

> The resurrection is not, as it were, a highly peculiar event within the present world (though it is that as well); it is, principally, the defining event of the new creation, the world which is being born with Jesus. If we are even to glimpse this world, let alone enter it, we will need a different kind of knowing, a knowing which draws out from us not just the cool appraisal of detached quasi-scientific research, but that whole-person engagement and involvement for which the best shorthand is "love", in the full Johannine sense of *agape*. (Tom Wright, *Surprised by Hope*, p. 84)

I am not unsympathetic to this suggestion of a different, lovingly engaged kind of knowing, but I suggest we should consider *what* we know in this way, and *how* we are supposed to know it.

Wittgenstein has such an awesome reputation as a philosopher that there is a danger of people treating his every word with more reverence than it may deserve. He was one of the 20th century's most original philosophers, ethnically Jewish but not practising Judaism, a passionate reader of the gospels and of Kierkegaard and Tolstoy who felt sympathy with Christian beliefs though he could not literally share them. I suspect he would be horrified to know that his private writings over many years have been published for scholars to pore over, under the pretentious (or ghastly?) title *Culture and Value: a selection from the posthumous remains*. (Some of them may reflect only his own idiosyncracies, or the prejudices of the time. There are, for example, some dubious remarks about "Jewishness" and music.) Still, his musings about resurrection are suggestive and provocative, so let us consider them with the questioning spirit that he encouraged in his students.

When Wittgenstein wrote "it is *love* that believes the Resurrection", did he mean that only loving people believe in the resurrection (of Jesus, and everyone)? — or that any truly loving person will believe in bodily resurrection? But both ways round seem obviously vulnerable to empirical counter-examples. So what was he getting at? Let us look at the context of this remark. The passage begins by noting that he was reading *1 Corinthians* 12:3: "No man can say that Jesus is the Lord, except by the Holy Ghost". Wittgenstein sees a truth in that: he admits that he himself cannot sincerely say "Jesus is Lord", because he does not believe that Jesus will come to judge him — and to believe that, he would have to live quite differently. His main point (also argued in the other main source for his philosophy of religion — the *Lectures and Conversations on Aesthetics, Psychology and Religious Belief*) is of course that religious affirmations go beyond assent to a theoretical proposition, for they commit the believer to a way of life. Here he asks himself "What inclines even me to believe in Christ's resurrection?" and he answers:

> If he did not rise from the dead ... he is a teacher, like any other, and can no longer help; and we are once more orphaned and alone. ... But if I am to be REALLY redeemed, — I need *certainty* — not wisdom, dreams, speculation — and this certainty is faith. And faith is what my *heart*, my soul, needs, not my speculative intellect. For my soul, with its passions, as it were with its flesh and blood, must be redeemed, not my abstract mind. (p. 38)

This may sound like Christian orthodoxy, reminiscent indeed of St. Paul saying "if Christ was not raised, then our gospel is null and void, and so is your faith". But what is to be the *content* of this faith, this passionate certainty? Is it that something beyond all scientific explanation happened to Jesus's body two thousand years ago? And that we will all be resurrected in bodily form, at the end of history? But *those* propositions would seem precisely to be matters for "the speculative intellect"; and why should intellectual assent to them be either necessary or sufficient for "redemption"? A few days earlier Wittgenstein had written:

> Christianity is not based on a historical truth, but presents us with a (historical) narrative and says: now believe! But not believe this report with the belief that is appropriate to a historical report,—but rather: believe, through thick and thin and you can do this only as the outcome of a life. *Here you have a message!—don't treat it as you would another historical message!* Make a *quite different* place for it in your life. (p. 37)
>
> Queer as it sounds; the historical accounts of the Gospels might, in the historical sense, be demonstrably false, and yet belief would lose nothing through this; but *not* because it has to do with "universal truths of reason"!—rather, because historical proof ... is irrelevant to belief. This message (the Gospels) is seized on by a human being believingly (i.e. lovingly). That is the certainty of this "taking-for-true", nothing *else*.
>
> The believer's relation to these messages is *neither* a relation to a historical truth (probability) *nor yet* to a doctrine consisting of "truths of reason". (pp. 37–8)

There is a clear anticipation of this in Kant's conception of *belief* or *faith* (his word 'Glaube' has been translated both ways) as held with a peculiarly subjective kind of certainty, distinct on the one hand from the objective certainty of *knowledge* in mathematics or empirical science, and on the other hand from *opinion*, where evidence is insufficient but could be supplemented and might then reach the standard of knowledge (*Critique of Pure Reason* A822/B850). In that passage Kant went on to say that no one can boast that he knows there is a God and a future life, but we can have *belief* or *faith* in them:

> ... the conviction is not *logical* but *moral* certainty, and, since it depends on subjective grounds (of moral disposition) I must not even say "*It is* morally certain that there is a God," etc., but rather "*I am* morally certain" etc. That is, the belief in God and another world is so interwoven with my moral disposition that I am in as little danger of ever surrendering the former as I am worried that the latter can ever be torn away from me. (A829/B857)

Here Kant the great apostle of reason seems to anticipate the Christian existentialism of Kierkegaard, who reacted against Enlightenment rationalism a couple of generations later.

But to which propositions should this attitude of passionate, subjectively certain, belief or faith be directed? The existence of God? The reality of life after death? The bodily resurrection of Christ? Or something completely different? In the passage just quoted and in the Dialectic section of his second *Critique (of Practical Reason)* Kant recommended God and immortality, but as we saw in Chapter 8, his later thought in the *Religion* became less definite on this, and he came to think that the really important thing—one's moral disposition—need not be so closely interwoven with any definite belief in God or an afterlife. Wittgenstein's talk of a historical narrative that should be believed but not with the *kind* of belief that is appropriate to a historical report is puzzling indeed—yet it seems to capture something that is peculiar about much religious belief. And he had some other suggestive thoughts about this:

> It is important that this narrative [i.e. the four gospels] should not have more than quite middling historical plausibility, *just so* that this should not be taken as the essential, decisive thing. So that the *letter* should not be believed more strongly than is proper and the *spirit* should receive its due, i.e. what you are supposed to see cannot be communicated even by the best, most accurate, historians; *therefore* a mediocre account suffices, is even to be preferred. ...
>
> The Spirit puts what is essential, essential for your life, into these words. The point is precisely that you are SUPPOSED to see clearly only what even *this* representation clearly shows. (pp. 36-7)

A little earlier, Wittgenstein wrote that in religious propositions "rules of life are dressed up in pictures" (p. 34)—which fits well with my case in Chapter 9.

Can one express such rules of life without the pictorial dressing, then?

Dare I suggest that there is an "inner", spiritual meaning about the belief in resurrection that is *concealed* by the "outer", apparently historical, form of words? The three Christian writers quoted above put the spiritual meaning in their own words, and I can hardly improve on them. Hugh Gilbert spoke of the "recognition of the presence of definitive salvation and ultimate good". Rowan Williams wrote of "a universal symbol, the focus and pivot of a fresh and transforming interpretation of all human reality", and of "a narrative structure in which we can locate our recovery of identity and human possibility". Michel Quenot affirmed that "creation has been freed and has found its essential meaning and its deepest unity".

It may be tempting to sum this by saying: "To believe in the Resurrection is to believe in the power of Love". But that kind of "A is B" formulation is ambiguous between "A implies B" and "A is nothing but B". Christians would surely agree that belief in the Resurrection *implies* belief in the power of love, but most of them would resist saying that the former *means only* the latter. I don't think this point should be glossed over: it is sometimes tempting to suggest that when people assert A they really mean only B, but if they reject that suggestion, we cannot make their words mean something different from what they are explicitly intended to mean. However my contention remains that B does not imply A, i.e. that one can believe, deeply and lovingly, in the power of love as a way of knowing people and indeed of transforming them for the better (think of the kind of love that Jesus showed for the people he met such as the woman taken in adultery, and that Socrates showed in his concern for the mental and moral well-being of his interlocutors) without having to believe in the bodily resurrection of Jesus or of the rest of us. May I end with a poem by Emily Dickinson:

> The blunder is to estimate—
> "Eternity is then",
> We say, as of a station.
> Meanwhile he is so near.
> He joins me in my ramble,
> Divides abode with me,
> No friend I have that so persists
> As this Eternity.

Further reading

Some New Testament scholars have questioned the historical reality of Jesus's bodily resurrection, such as G. Ludemann, *The Resurrection of Jesus* (London: SCM Press 1995), and A.J.M. Wedderburn, *Beyond Resurrection* (London: SCM Press 1999). They have of course been resolutely opposed, for example by Tom Wright, in *Surprised by Hope* (London: SPCK 2007).

The three Christian writers I quoted on the resurrection are:

Dom Hugh Gilbert, *Unfolding the Mystery: Monastic Conferences on the Liturgical Year* (Leominster: Gracewing 2007);

Rowan Williams, *Resurrection: Interpreting the Easter Gospel* (London: Darton, Longman and Todd, 1982, revised edition 2002);

Michel Quenot, *The Resurrection and the Icon* (Crestwood: St.Vladimir's Seminary Press 1997).

Ludwig Wittgenstein, *Culture and Value: A Selection from the Posthumous Remains*, revised second edition (Oxford: Blackwell 1998) — follow the index references to belief/faith, Christianity, God, and religion. See also Wittgenstein's *Lectures and Conversations on Aesthetics, Psychology and Religious Belief*, edited by Cyril Barrett (Oxford: Blackwell 1966).

Books on spirituality and philosophy of religion that have impressed me include:

Leszek Kolakowski, *Religion* (St.Augustine's Press 1982)

Stewart R. Sutherland, *God, Jesus and Belief* (Oxford: Blackwell 1984)

David Walsh, *Guarded by Mystery: Meaning in a Postmodern Age* (Washington: The Catholic University of America Press 1999)

Michael McGhee, *Transformations of Mind: Philosophy as Spiritual Practice* (Cambridge University Press 2000)

John Cottingham, *The Spiritual Dimension: Religion, Philosophy and Human Value* (Cambridge University Press 2005)

INDEX

Abelard 81
Abraham 23, 28, 31, 70
Alcibiades 15-16
Alexander the Great 25, 45, 49
Al-Ghazali 75-6, 119
Al-Hallaj 74
Alkaios 147
Allen, Beth 151
Ambler, Rex 150
Anabaptists 87
Anan 78
Anaxogoras 11
Anglicanism 87-8, 91, 94, 100, 110, 115, 146
Antiochus 25
Apocalypse 41-2, 62-3
Aquinas 81-2, 144, 146, 161
Aristophanes 12
Aristotle 5, 10, 45, 48-50, 74, 76-8, 81-2, 85, 116, 160-1
Atonement 61, 130
Augustine 7, 48, 67, 103, 119, 124, 125

Baptists 89
Barclay, Robert 100, 104-8, 111
Beauty 132-3
Bernard of Clairveaux 81
Blake, William 140, 141
Buddhism 2, 5, 113, 148, 151, 158

Burnell, Jocelyn 170
Burns, Robert 1
Byrne, Peter 143
Byzantium 68, 80, 141

Callicles 19
Calvin, John 86
Carter, Jimmy 37
Cathars 80
Charles II 96, 99-100, 104
Cleanthes 52-3
Confucianism 2, 5, 113
Constantine 65-8
Cromwell, Oliver 88-9, 99

Dalai Lama 158
Daniel 26, 41
Dante 161
David 24-5, 28
Darwin, Charles 115, 149, 152
Descartes, Rene 106-7, 160
Dickinson, Emily 177
Doncaster, L.Hugh 109, 128
Durant, Will 60

Eastern Orthodoxy 67-9, 115, 140-1, 172
Eckhardt, Meister 144
Eddington, Arthur 127-8
Eliot, T.S. 5

Enlightenment 5, 85, 112-18, 124, 165, 175
Enthusiasm 111-14, 121, 130
Epictetus 55
Epicureanism 45, 50-2, 55
Epistemology 43, 109-113, 119, 127-8, 165, 173-7
Essenes 26
Ethics 3, 10-21, 34-8, 42-3, 49, 51
Euripides 11
Evil 61, 123-5, 149, 165
Existentialism 120

Faith 31, 43-4, 111, 113-14, 119, 123, 128, 141, 154, 164-5, 174-6
Family 2, 35, 38-9
Farrer, Austin 110-111, 145-9, 152
Fell, Margaret 98
Forgiveness 34-5, 42, 86, 149, 170
Fox, George 67, 85-101, 105, 123, 159
Frankfurt, Harry 7
Frederick the Great 118
Frederick William II 119
Freewill 50, 53, 86, 118, 120, 124-6, 132, 145, 152, 162-4
Freud, Sigmund 5

Gilbert, Hugh 170, 176
Gillman, Harvey 127
Gnosticism 63-4
Grace 6, 62, 86, 126, 129-30
Graveson, Caroline 132-3

Handel 26
Hasidism 80
Hawel, Vaclav 151
Holy Spirit 59-60, 63-4, 67-9, 92-101, 103, 105-113, 126, 131, 136, 139, 152, 168, 172, 174-6

Homer 138
Hope 26, 40, 56, 111, 123
Hopkins, Gerard Manley 133
Housman, A.E. 146
Hume, David 112-13, 117, 148
Hyperbole 35-6

Ideals 2-7, 35, 121
Ibn-Rushd 76-9, 81, 144, 161
Ibn-Sina 75, 77, 144, 161
Incarnation 29-30, 59-61, 63-4, 66, 123, 125, 139-40
Irenaeus 63-5
Isaiah 26, 56, 70
Islam 59, 66-7, 70-8, 80-1, 83, 115, 117, 131, 135, 139-40, 157-8, 161, 166

James II 100
Jesus 1-2, 12, 19, 21, 23-44, 45, 59, 70-72, 78, 80, 89, 94, 113, 123, 128, 130, 139, 157, 159,160, 162, 165-8, 177
John 29-31, 48, 61, 63, 105, 139
Jones, Rufus 133
Joshua 23
Judaism 23-27, 29-30, 37-8, 52, 59-61, 66-7, 77-81, 83, 115, 117, 131, 135, 157-8, 161, 166
Justin Martyr 64
Justinian 56

Kabbalah 79
Kant, Immanuel 112, 114, 116-133, 144, 148, 154, 175-6
Karaites 78
Kierkegaard, Soren 119, 175

Lampen, John 149
Lash, Nicholas 143

INDEX

Levellers 89
Lewis, C.S. 5, 7
Light 87, 92-101, 103-113, 126, 136, 153, 159
Locke, John 111-114, 121, 130
Lonsdale, Kathleen 128
Love 2, 5, 15-16, 33-5, 42, 47, 62, 71, 86, 111, 128-9, 136, 145, 149, 162, 168, 173-7
Lucretius 54
Luke 28
Luther 85-6, 125

Maccabees 25-6
Macmurray, John 133
Maimonedes 78-9, 144, 161
Marcus Aurlelius 54-6
Mark 27-8
Mary 28, 60, 70, 80, 131, 165
Matthew 28
McFague, Sallie 142-3
Metaphors 30, 52, 75-7, 120, 127, 135-154, 168-9
Michelangelo 140
Miracles 31, 113, 121, 131, 165
Moore, Gareth 155
Morality 2-7, 10-21, 46-7, 52, 119-120, 123-5, 129
Moses 23, 98, 113, 137, 140, 157
Muhammad 70-3, 75-7, 80, 157-8
Murdoch, Iris 152
Mysticism 63, 74, 79-80, 82, 131, 132, 144

Nayler, James 97-8

Origen 46, 65, 78, 144

Pagels, Elaine 30, 63-4
Pascal, Blaise 119

Paul 6, 19, 21, 27, 61-3, 67, 139, 160, 169
Pelagius 125
Penn, William 100, 103
Peter 28, 59, 61
Pharisees 26, 37, 39
Philo 48, 52
Pietism 118
Pilate 26-7
Plantinga, Alvin 142
Plato 5, 10-12, 15, 20, 31, 42, 45-50, 61, 81, 103, 116, 147, 152, 160-1
Plotinus 48, 103
Popper, Karl 107
Protagoras 10, 11, 17-18
Prudence 1-7, 36
Pseudo-Dionysius 144

Quakerism 64, 69, 86-101, 108-9, 114, 120-133, 136, 144, 149-51, 153, 159-160
Quenot, Michel 172, 176

Reformation 66, 85-7, 115, 130, 158
Reid, Thomas 117
Renaissance 85
Resurrection 25, 27, 42, 59-61, 75, 79, 126, 128, 160-177
Roman Catholicism 66, 85, 108, 158
Roman Empire 1, 26-7, 32, 39, 45-6, 53-6, 59-62, 64-6
Rountree, William 130
Rumi 74-5

Saadia 78
Sadducees 25, 160
Samaritans 25, 34, 36, 40
Sartre, Jean-Paul 120, 164
Schopenhauer, Arthur 5
Science 68-9, 85, 88, 94, 106, 113-14, 118, 143, 145, 149, 150, 165

Seneca 55
Shakespeare, William 1, 85, 88, 95
Socrates 5, 9-22, 31, 33-4, 38, 42-3, 45-7, 61, 89, 118, 177
Solomon 24
Sophists 10
Soul 16-17, 19-20, 46, 49, 51-2, 82, 118-19, 132, 146-8, 160-1
Stoicism 45, 51-2, 55-6, 62
Sufism 74-6, 79, 144
Swinburne, Richard 142
Sutherland, Stuart 140, 156

Tertullian 46, 64-5, 75
Thackeray, William 4
Thatcher, Margaret 36
Tiepelo 141
Thomas 30, 32-3, 63
Tolstoy, Leo 5, 173
Traditions 4, 6-7, 43, 74, 82-3, 121-3, 135-6, 153-4, 157-9, 164-5

Trinity 67-8, 81, 100-101, 105, 140, 153

Unitarians 123

Williams, Rowan 170, 176
Wisdom 25, 47-56, 138
Wittgenstein, Ludwig 20, 140, 153-4, 173--6
Women 40-41, 51, 62, 65, 91
Wordsworth, William 133, 156
Wright, Tom 164, 173

Xenophon 12, 61

Zealots 26-7
Zeno 51
Zeus 18, 52-3
Zohar 144
Zwingli 86